ALSO BY AMY LEACH

The Everybody Ensemble

Things That Are

The

SALT

of the

UNIVERSE

The

SALT

of the

UNIVERSE

Praise, Songs, and
Improvisations

AMY LEACH

FARRAR, STRAUS AND GIROUX

NEW YORK

Farrar, Straus and Giroux
120 Broadway, New York 10271

Library of Congress Cataloging-in-Publication Data
Names: Leach, Amy, 1975– author.
Title: The salt of the universe : praise, songs, and improvisations /
    Amy Leach.
Description: First edition. | New York : Farrar, Straus and Giroux,
    2024.
Identifiers: LCCN 2023059576 | ISBN 9780374607920 (hardcover)
Subjects: LCSH: Dogma. | LCGFT: Creative nonfiction. | Essays.
Classification: LCC PS3612.E21275 S25 2024 | DDC 814/.6—dc23/
    eng/20240102
LC record available at https://lccn.loc.gov/2023059576

Designed by Gretchen Achilles

Our books may be purchased in bulk for promotional,
educational, or business use. Please contact your local bookseller
or the Macmillan Corporate and Premium Sales Department at
1-800-221-7945, extension 5442, or by email at
MacmillanSpecialMarkets@macmillan.com.

www.fsgbooks.com
Follow us on social media at @fsgbooks

1 3 5 7 9 10 8 6 4 2

For Peter and Sylvie

Salt is good, but if it loses its saltiness,
how can you make it salty again?

—JESUS

Do not eat largely of salt; give up bottled
pickles.

—ELLEN G. WHITE

Contents

CONTENTS

PART III

PART IV

Preface

I don't know how it works on other planets but on Earth the necessary is always turning into the superfluous. Our necessary skill of talking has evolved into superfluities like sonnets and scatting and doo-wopping and operettas. Sleep turns into dreaming, walking turns into tangoing, pogoing, limboing, funk. Recently I saw people who seemed to have given up walking altogether, who appeared to *only dance*. I played the piano for a ballroom dance and was as bewitched as I would be if the pile of laundry in my basement were to get up and start dancing, the black pants with golden bees on them pirouetting, the blue snowflake socks foxtrotting around the basement floor, the beige trench coat swaying with its arms wrapped around the frilly pink-and-green peasant dress. Playing for a ballroom dance feels like trying not to watch the laundry dancing: if I looked up from my chord charts I got flipped like a boat and had no clue which measure we were on in "La Isla Bonita."

Imagine the laundry being possessed—but, of course, it *is* possessed, when we wear it, and to observe a ballroom dance is precisely to see the laundry dancing, shiny bronze dresses sashaying with pressed white shirts, etc. I've seen funeral clothes bouncing around: I'd prepared somber piano music for the memorial service but when I arrived they asked for boogie-woogie. I've seen onesies bobbing, jammies twirling, waving their arms in the air, even if the music was just "Twinkle Twinkle," not the song with the most diggable beat, we're not talking Tito Puente.

The amusement of dancing, as conducted at the present day, is a school of depravity, a fearful curse to society. If all in our great cities who are yearly ruined by this means could be brought together, what histories of wrecked lives would be revealed.

So declared Ellen G. White, the founding prophet of the Seventh-day Adventist Church, the church in which I grew up. To follow her commandments, to prevent the wrecking and ruining of lives, Adventist schools historically held Grand Marches instead of dances, with boys and girls marching around a field in opposite directions and nobody going off on tangents, nobody busting a move, and I imagine being able to accompany *those* events no problem. I imagine being able to keep my eyes off the regulation skirts and pants marching around in regulation circles, but maybe not off the trees across the field, blowing in a frenzy, nor off the clouds skittering across the sky.

Jesus told a parable where it's not dancing but *non-dancing* that's the problem. There are children singing and playing the flute and nobody is responding, and the children complain:

> *We played the flute for you,*
> *and you did not dance;*
> *we sang a dirge,*
> *and you did not mourn.*

How grim not to dance when children play the flute, how mean not to cry when they sing a sad song. Sometimes there is nothing so hard as a heart.

Judging from this story, Jesus understood that there is a difference between a song and a song—there are crying songs and dancing songs. And judging from the wine he conjured at that one wedding, the fine wine that shocked everyone after the plonk they'd been drinking, he also understood there is a difference between a grape and a grape. Just as there is a difference between a song and a song and a grape and a grape, so is there a difference between a fish and a fish, a fiddler and a fiddler, a soul and a soul, and wouldn't it be weird if every soul told the same story, recited the same script, sang the same song, marched around the same regulated circuit?

William James celebrated variation between souls. In *The Varieties of Religious Experience* James lets the mystic souls, the healthy-minded souls, and the melancholy souls all speak for themselves. He quotes, at length, Walt Whitman, Martin Luther, Leo Tolstoy, "a patient in a French asylum," a Muslim gentleman, a Nova Scotian evangelist, and "an active and useful rescuer of drunkards in New York," among many other idiosyncratic souls, as they recount their own religious experience.

Now, in this book, I will let my soul speak for itself. You may have heard of the "unchurched" but I am the "overchurched": I figure I've heard about five thousand sermons in my life, and now, after all that sitting and listening, I have something to say too. I wish to speak from my own soul, my own gizzard, my own experience, and to tell how experience danced me out of the regulated march of fundamentalism.

To borrow the words of an old hymn: "This is my story, this is my song."

PART I

*

By all means they try to hold me
secure who love me in this world.
But it is otherwise with thy love,
which is greater than theirs, and
thou keepest me free.

—RABINDRANATH TAGORE

Man is tormented by no greater
anxiety than to find someone
quickly to whom he can hand over
that great gift of freedom with
which the ill-fated creature is born.

—FYODOR DOSTOYEVSKY

The Answer Book

Fundamentalists love rules. I used to be a fundamentalist fiddler. When first I went from playing the violin in an orchestra to playing the fiddle with a bluegrass band, I had a list of rules for myself, all subtractive: don't play clean, don't play pretty-pretty, and never play busy-busy while the singer is singing. The rigidity of my rules came from my lack of experience, and I strictly adhered to them, playing my nonclean, nonpretty, nonbusy parts—until one day I listened to a song by a bluegrass band whose fiddler flouted every one of my rules. That was the day my fiddle fundamentalism gave way to freedom, and I am no longer a fuddy-duddy fiddler.

German and Russian composers, Spanish and Hungarian composers—all of them write their performance instructions in Italian. *Pomposo* means "pompous," *strepitoso* means "noisy," *dolce* means "sweet," *stringendo* means "increasing in speed." The performer can be obediently pompous, obediently sweet, obediently noisy, and she can obediently accelerate. However, it is harder to obey this instruction—*liberamente*. How can one be obediently free? It appears that many musicians have asked the internet this question: "What does 'freely' mean?"

Autonomy can feel confusing, like somebody's playing a joke on you, somebody like Erik Satie, the composer who wrote the following performance instructions on one of his piano pieces: "Comme un rossignol qui aurait mal aux dents"—which means "Like a nightingale with a toothache." Some of Satie's other directions tell the pianist to play "a little bloody" or "dry like a cuckoo," or to "put your hand in your pocket." He instructs you to play a certain section "840 times," and in another place you are to play the notes "in your head." The obedient pianist is not amused.

Obedient persons just generally are not amused by freedom, by autonomy: *Autonomy's a prank, autonomy's an affliction, and if we could only figure out who the afflicter is, boy, would we give him a piece of our minds!* Many institutions provide a cure for this affliction: dogma. Dogma is a vise in whose jaws you are free from being free. Dogma obviates the need for a conscience or a brain. It seems funny that the animals with the most brainpower are the animals eagerest to put their brains in a vise. From what I've seen of sloths, I do not think they go around thinking, "Put me in a vise" like humans do—"Put me in a vise, tell me what to do, what to think, what to say, what to eat, what to drink, what not to eat and not to drink and not to read and not to think." Sloths, being disinclined to subordinate themselves, are rarely targets of evangelistic campaigns or political propaganda. Sloths are unsuitable subordinates.

Of course for some people obedience is not an impulse but an obligation. Claudio Monteverdi's son Massimiliano, a physician, was imprisoned by inquisitors because he was accused of owning a prohibited book. If his father hadn't sold a necklace for one hundred ducats so he could pay the Father Inquisitor to get his son out of prison, Massimiliano might have been put on the rack for it. The Monteverdis were accidentally—not temperamentally—obedient.

There is a distinction to be made between one's accidental identity and one's temperamental identity. Accidentally I live in Montana but temperamentally I am tropical. I am accidentally a laundrywoman but temperamentally an aristocrat. I know someone who is accidentally a person but temperamentally a panda bear and I have met people who temperamentally seem to be potatoes. I also know one small, curly-haired, dainty-looking girl who is mule-mettled.

The institutions one was born into may or may not correspond to one's temperament. Some accidental fundamentalists are temperamentally loosey-goosey, and other people, born into a loosey-gooseyer context, are fundamentally fundamentalists—give them scripts to recite, answers, rules, regulations, strictures, prohibitions, uniforms, marching orders. More interesting, to me, than the accidental identity is the temperamental one, the one you can hear when somebody sings.

Some accidentally subjugated folks are temperamentally free and some accidentally free persons are temperamentally subservient: even if they live in a democracy, they have the hots for despots. In 1776, while some people were writing the Declaration of Independence, other folks got busy drafting a Declaration of Dependence, the gist of which is: autonomy's a drag. Five hundred and forty-seven Loyalists signed a document that pledged allegiance to the king of England and denounced "the most unnatural, unprovoked Rebellion, that ever disgraced the annals of Time."

* * *

The members of a democracy are called citizens, not subjects—but the subjects of a book are always called subjects. Books are dictatorships, not democracies. Sometimes when I am reading a book I start wishing the subjects would rebel—rise up and depose the author—but with other books I do not think this. These are the less authoritarian authors, the more Shakespearean ones. As Hegel said, Shakespeare's characters are "free artists of themselves."

But even those of us lucky enough to be citizens of a democracy are still subjects of time, compared with whom Stalin was a softie. You can beg for mercy, plead with time for time, but time will give no quarter. Time's a tyrant, ironhanded.

But oh well, what's a subversive temperament for, if not subverting tyrants? Are we going to go around subverting daffodils? One of my favorite ways of sub-verting time is to read old books. Although I was born in the twentieth century, I grew up in a house full of seventeenth-century books, nineteenth-century books, so instead of reading new serious books I read old funny books. Another way of subverting time is to write "poor rhymes" like Shakespeare—"I'll live in this poor rhyme."

Those of us who cannot write poor rhymes like Shake-speare might have children. The twentieth century was a heavy one but I had children who simply sidestepped it. One can also subvert time by living in the past, by writing one's memoirs. When I am dead I will live in the past—I will write my memoir about being alive, about collecting ladybugs in my lunch box in the cornfield be-hind our house in Colorado when I was five, about sitting in a van when I was in high school, waiting to go who knows where, about catching glimpses of my dogs running themselves silly in the Chicago forest, about holding a sturdy baby and watching the icicles hanging outside the window melting drop by drop.

For these repetitive, prolonged, uneventful experiences are what I remember most. If, once, I participated in a swimming contest in the icy ocean, and was dragged to the bottom by a water beast, and I swam to the surface and bludgeoned nine sea monsters, I have forgotten it all. But I do remember biking fifty miles into the wind on a little Texas road when I was eleven. The wind was so fierce, the ride so slow and laborious, that this many years on, I suspect I am still riding that heavy pink Huffy into the hot summer wind, and that all the intervening days are provisional, unconvincingly appended.

In my posthumous memoir there will be no chapters about sports. If anyone should ever have contracted the sports bug, it was me, from being exposed daily as a child. But to this normally contagious condition I proved unusually resistant. Like someone infested with rodents and fleas who never suffers the plague, I have never been able to register a single play of football, baseball, basketball, or any other ball. If I happen to be in a room where there's a game on TV, I feel my eyes drifting to the ceiling.

The only times I ever registered the existence of footballs were when they were thrown down my tuba in band class. It was not hubris, as a fifth grader, to choose the tuba as my band instrument, but a joke, my physique being in such contrast to the instrument's physique. If I had been sizable I would have played the piccolo. The tuba was the joke that taught me how a joke can turn into a joke on yourself, how a joke can turn into fate, dented and ponderous and drippy with spit.

My joke became my fate for twelve years because I lived in a small town and small towns hold you to your instrument. For a town to be able to march with dignity, they can't have their kids switching instruments all over the place. The good thing about playing the tuba is that it is difficult to be sentimental on it—*oompah, oompah, oompah-pah*. The bad thing about playing the tuba is that it is hard to translate your own experience into tuba music, especially when footballs are occluding it.

As immune as I am to sports, I am equally immune to the apocalypse, though this resistance was differently acquired. I am inherently immune to sports but received an apocalypse inoculation: from sustained suffering and subsequent recovery I have strong antibodies. According to my Seventh-day Adventist teachers, the world was going to end before I finished first grade, then fourth grade, then sixth grade, and I was very susceptible, always in a tizzy, till I wasn't, until I called the apocalypse's bluff. It was always tardy, always wasting my time, and anyway the prognosticators were always passing away.

There was the teacher who told us first graders that the Jesuits were going to line our families up against a wall and shoot our parents in the head if we did not renounce the seventh-day Sabbath. (But if we did renounce the Sabbath we wouldn't go to heaven.) There was the teacher who whenever helicopters flew over our school told us it was the Jesuits surveilling us. There was the teacher who always wore a fanny pack full of energy gels, plus water purification tablets, plus a space blanket for the impending hour when the Jesuits would arrive to torture us—*RUN!* The imminent persecution by Catholics was called the Time of Trouble, which presaged the Second Coming.

But anyway I can prognosticate, too, and I prognosticate: no apocalypse. For while the apocalypse is sexy short-term, long-term it's a slog. What I resent about the apocalypse is that it makes people sacrificially practical: everything plays second fiddle to the apocalypse, including fiddles. If time is short, there is no time for fiddling (or yodeling). I knew a cellist—she was the cat's pajamas—but, believing the end was near, she relinquished her cello and became a dental hygienist missionary, cleaning teeth against the last day. While hygiene is a good cause and I am glad for hygienists to become hygienists, I still want cellists to become cellists, even if (or especially if) time is short. With the cellists and the tufted puffins, I defy augury.

Uncertainty cannot see very far but certainty can see no farther. In 1844 there were around one hundred thousand believers who were 100 percent certain Jesus was coming back on October 22. William Miller and his many Millerites quit their jobs, divested themselves of all their possessions, climbed New England hills, and waited for Jesus to appear. Jesus conspicuously did not appear. (Usually he inconspicuously does not appear.) It was a disappointing day; they called it the Great Disappointment. But I have wondered if even more disappointing than Jesus not showing up was the disappointment of being divested of their one remaining possession, their most cherished one—the possession they never would have relinquished.

If you happen to live near a religious relinquisher, then you know how fun it is to set up a lawn chair nearby and watch the show. Here come the whiskey and tequila and cigarettes flying out the window, the snuff and the pork, the jewelry, novels, drums, and television, all piling up in the yard with some boyfriends landing on top. If you watch long enough you'll eventually see the world sailing out the window, too, thudding onto the lawn, slowly rolling away.

There is, however, one thing you will never see sailing out a relinquisher's window. Though the Millerites cheerfully jettisoned their wagons and plows, hammers and hats, spoons and suspenders, they held on with a death grip to one last thing, the one thing that, on October 22, 1844, was wrenched out of their hands: their certainty. It is hard enough on the certain person when he is forced, over *years*, to become an uncertain person. Imagine it happening all in one day.

After the Great Disappointment came the aftermath—the ensuing days—October 23, October 24, October 25, etc., and with the aftermath came the memoirs. (Memoirs always accompany aftermath.) William Miller's memoir describes the patriotism of his father and the presentiments of his mother—unmistakable presentiments like tornadoes bearing down on bland little birds. It describes Miller's punishing schedule on the lecture circuit and his being called "unhandsome appellations," and it describes his rival lecturer Abner Kneeland, who unscrupulously supplemented his theological talks with "protracted dances." William Miller never would have done that.

William Miller's memoir was written by someone named Sylvester Bliss. Now, I went to memoir school but my professors never told me you can write *somebody else's memoir*. We were all expected to write *our own memoirs* but I was not in the mood to write my own memoir. I would have been much more excited if I had known you can write someone else's. I would have written the memoir of one of those porcupine ancestors who rafted across the ocean forty million years ago: *I could already feel my babies bobbling around inside me when I got swept onto the raft. If I had known the ocean was going to be so big, I would have abandoned the raft and paddled for shore. As it happened, all my little red fuzzy-furred porcupettes were born at sea.*

Personally, I am not disappointed that Jesus did not come back in 1844. For me it would have been the Great Disappointment if he *had* come back, because then I wouldn't have gotten to exist and I would always have wondered what it was like to exist. As it was, I had been wondering for eons—you have *no idea* how many eons there were leading up to 1975.

Jesus's return would also have been disappointing since all Felix Mendelssohn's efforts on his violin concerto would have been in vain. Because, from 1838 to 1844, while those New Englanders were getting ready to leave the planet, Mendelssohn was composing his Violin Concerto in E minor. In 1838 he wrote to a friend in Leipzig, "I would like to write you a violin concerto for next winter as well; I have one in E minor in my head, the opening leaves me no peace." He was not one of those piners for the end: he had a concerto in his head. My theory is that the apocalypse appeals primarily to people who have no

13

concerto in their heads, and personally, I'd rather be like Mr. Mendelssohn than Mr. Miller. The apocalypse can't be had for the hankering but the concerto sometimes can.

* * *

There's an old Russian story, "The Soldier's Tale," in which a soldier returning home from war gives his violin to the devil, in return for a book that contains all the answers. The violin is actually his soul: in exchange for the answer book, the soldier gives away his soul. To help pay my tuition in high school I used to go door-to-door selling an Adventist book that similarly claimed to have all the answers, though we charged only ten dollars for it. But riding in the back of the van on the way to different Denver neighborhoods, I would read the vaunted book and notice that the questions seemed engineered, finagled, formulated, as if the authors had *started* with the answers (Bible texts) and then made up questions to fit them. There was not a single stumper in there.

Also it never addressed questions like how can birds eat habanero peppers or what is a muon or why do some flammulated owls fly all the way from El Salvador to British Columbia and back every year while other flammulated owls just stay in Oaxaca or why did Conway Twitty's personality change in 1981 or who lives in that one house on Little Island in the middle of Lake Chargoggagoggmanchauggagoggchaubunagungamaugg? If that book answered all one's questions, one did not have very many questions.

The violin is a vehicle for the soul and one may exchange it for all the answers, but according to that folktale it is not God but the devil who peddles answers at such a premium. Jesus himself wasn't all that forthcoming—deflecting, deflecting, like Hamlet, answering questions not with answers but with questions and parables, expressly so that people would not understand.

A premature answer can preclude experience, and experience, if you make accommodations to it, can teach you a lot. For example, you might be only ten pillows—or ten apocalyptic sermons—away from realizing you don't enjoy being smothered. Hold out for experience, little boy; hold on to your fiddle, little girl. To not get swindled of your fiddle is to not get swindled of your soul.

Temperamental identities. There are all kinds of characters running around in human suits, just as there are all kinds of characters running around in hamster suits. We used to have one hamster who hissed at us and hid in his tube if we came near his cage, and another hamster who, whenever we approached her cage, ran over and climbed her wire wall to be as close to us as possible. Now we have a hamster who scampers down our legs onto the floor, and an opposite hamster who scuttles up our arms, onto our shoulders, onto the tops of our heads: we have a down-hamster and an up-hamster.

A concerto in the head. Having a baby in the uterus is as good as having a concerto in the head for becoming disenchanted with the apocalypse. Being great with child is as good as being great with song. Though Jesus did not appear in 1844, Gerard Manley Hopkins did, and I bet his mother, Catherine, was the opposite of disappointed! Of course sometimes in the middle of his life, Gerard Manley's birth was a great disappointment to himself.

A concerto in the head. I wish I had a concerto in my head instead of Phil Collins's "A Groovy Kind of Love," which has been stuck in my head for approximately thirty years now.

The apocalypse is sexy. "The End Is Nigh" makes for a sexier sandwich board than "The Middle Is Nigh."

Jesuits. The Jesuits were supposedly obsessed with us Adventists, obsessed enough to hire helicopters in which to hover over our little school. However, it seems to me that the obsession ran in the other direction.

Memoirs. Memoirists in their twenties are often criticized for writing memoirs at such an inexperienced age. But if all memoirists were supposed to wait sixty years before they wrote their memoirs, that would preclude the jellyfish memoirs. It is always helpful to keep jellyfish in mind when thinking through a truism.

Memoirs. The material of memoirs is memories. Mostly what I remember is songs—but not the words, just the tunes—so if I wrote a memoir, it would be mostly me humming tunes, tunes tunes tunes, tuney tunes tunes, *hmm-mmmm-hmm-mm-mm-hmmm.*

The world sailing out the window. If you throw the world out the window, it might roll into the road and get run over by a bus. Some people would indeed throw the world under the bus.

Adventists Are
Like People

Once, I was only sixteen Mormons away from discovering that Mormons are heterogeneous. I took an ethnography class in graduate school and chose Mormons as my subject because I had heard them called homogeneous and wanted to find out if that was true: I would take my question to them personally. I asked Mark, "Mark, are you homogeneous?" and he said he was not; and I asked Marjorie, "Marjorie, are *you* homogeneous?" and she assured me that no, she was not homogeneous; and from the other interviews I conducted, and also from going on a hayride with a bunch of heterogeneous Mormons, I concluded, in my final essay, that Mormons are like people.

Probably if I had chosen to do my ethnographic research on "men" or "magicians" my conclusion would have been the same—men are like people, magicians are like people. If I had studied beauty queens or hillbillies or Jesuits or the population that lives along the Banana River or speakers of the Mecklenburgisch-Vorpommersch dialect or even soldiers, for whom homogeneity is an ideal, I think all my essays would have had the same thesis. I think I would have been a one-theory ethnographer.

"I hate Adventists," a Unitarian minister once told me, when I told her I had grown up Seventh-day Adventist. But she might as well have said, *I hate people*, because Adventists are like people: some are like sheep and some are like goats. Some are submissive and some are subversive; some are good regurgitators while others are not. Some Adventists are apocalypse-happy, some are apocalypse-sad, and others are apocalypse-indifferent. Some keep their minds on the Second Coming and some keep their minds on money and some are distractible by shooting stars.

But anyway it is apparently okay to hate people as long as you hate them in sections: one time I sat down in a fancy restaurant with some academics who, when I said I was from Texas, declared, "I hate Texas" and "I hate Texans" and "I do too." Of course their problem, like the Unitarian minister's problem, was that they had never met my grandfather, an autonomous heterogeneous subversive Adventist Texan who did *not* hate people, even in sections. He told my brother and me, when we were little, that he liked us because we reminded him of people.

Prophets are like people too; they come in all stripes; you've got your power prophets and polygamist prophets, moony prophets and miserabilist prophets; you've got your golden-bird prophets and poop-eating prophets and William Blake, who as a child saw angels gallivanting in the trees. There's Mr. Quimby with his Quimbyists and Mr. Flurry with his Flurryists and Ellen G. White, who counseled her followers to never, ever resort to eating pickles. Ellen White was the prophet assigned to me, but as soon as I could I exchanged her for Emily Dickinson.

Along with the memoirs, another aftermath of the Great Disappointment was Seventh-day Adventism. Now, I have recently learned that the "math" part of "aftermath" does not mean "math" but "mowing," which makes more sense—because after I say some math, like "The product of six to the third power and four times four is three thousand four hundred and fifty-six," nothing seems to follow that. However, when I mow the lawn, all kinds of things happen afterward: the grass grows back, the aspen sprouts reappear, the thistles return. One summer my mother-in-law spent a whole week digging up every wicked little thistle in my yard, and two weeks later the thousands of thistles were back, and that is aftermath.

After the Millerites' certainty was mown down, their certainty grew back, and many of them became Seventh-day Adventists. Maybe certainty is more a matter of temperament than anything else and maybe it is impossible to relinquish your temperament. Maybe the certain person cannot truly become uncertain. After Jesus did not show up in 1844, Ellen White simply displaced the whole scheme and had Jesus arriving not at *Planet Earth* on October 22 but at *Planet Neptune.*

Just kidding: she actually had him arriving that day at an office in heaven, where he started doing clerical work. One way to save face if your prophecy doesn't come true is to say it did come true but somewhere the minions can't see—Manitoba, Pondicherry, paradise. My problem with this scenario is not that it is too invisible but that it is not invisible enough—so if you had enough fuel you could rocket up to heaven and see Jesus secretarially bent over his ledgers, tallying up everyone's pickle infractions. *There are fewer things in heaven and earth, Horatio, than are dreamt of in your philosophy.*

I guess if you have no pull you have to push. Our moon, the moon, being so big, does not need to come down and push the ocean around, but a mini-moon would have to do that. I prefer pully moons to pushy moons, and pully people to pushy people. Ellen White was a very pushy prophet compared with Emily Dickinson hiding behind her hyacinths. Ellen White was also very verbose in comparison with Emily Dickinson—boy, will she give you an earful. But the funny thing is that Ellen White *led* me to Emily Dickinson. I was teaching literature at an Adventist college in California that followed Mrs. White's injunctions against reading fiction, and so I omitted the novels and stories I normally would have taught and instead taught poetry by Emily Dickinson, word ninja. And I realized that although I do not like to be pushed, I really like to be pulled.

* * *

Jesus conspicuously did not appear in the sky in 1844, but he did appear inconspicuously in a manger in 1 or so. To this inconspicuous appearance there were both public and private responses. The angels and shepherds and Anna and Simeon got all public and noisy about it, but while they were busily broadcasting the news, "Mary kept all these things and pondered them in her heart." Amid all that noisiness and newsiness, the person closest to the baby kept quiet.

(To this day Jesus has some very public, very vociferous followers. I would never tell them my secrets. I wonder if he still wishes they would be less vociferous. "But thou, when thou prayest, enter into thy closet, and when thou hast shut thy door, pray to thy Father which is in secret . . .")

Emily Dickinson grew up in a church where everybody was supposed to be a loudmouth like the angels and nobody was supposed to be a ponderer like Mary. Because she would not stand up and publicly confess her faith,

Dickinson was deemed a "no-hoper." Mary Lyon, the head of Mount Holyoke Female Seminary, where Dickinson was attending school, had "asked all those who wanted to be Christians to rise." Emily didn't stand up. As Clara Newman Turner later reported Emily's description of the event: "'They thought it queer I didn't rise'—adding with a twinkle in her eye, 'I thought a lie would be queerer.'" Even as a teenager, Emily Dickinson was no crumpler to pressure—and her resistance served her poetry well. Public poets have to be careful about what they say—careful, nervous, shrewd, and responsible, like politician poets—but recluses can be reckless, like four-year-olds.

* * *

In the green grass by the bend in a stream, my four-year-old found a stone, flat and round. She took a piece of snake grass, dipped it into the stream, and wrote a message on the stone. A piece of snake grass looks like a slim segmented pen with a pointy tip. What does someone write who cannot spell and has not yet been programmed? She would not tell me, and neither could I read the messages of all the other four-year-olds who had written on that same stone, back through the ages, with snake grass for pens and water for ink.

Within you, within you, the Kingdom of God is within you.

*

Fewer things in heaven and earth. Hamlet said to Horatio, "There are more things in heaven and earth, Horatio, than are dreamt of in your philosophy." But some books and some churches make me feel that there are *fewer* things in heaven and earth than I had dreamed possible.

Private/public. Usually it seems preferable to be private instead of public, but if I were a bison I'd rather be a public bison, because the private bison are always getting ground up and turned into burgers.

No-hoper. Most of us are no-hopers in one area or another, like snake-charming, cliff-jumping, truck-fixing, stage-diving, or house-keeping, and some of us are no-hopers, no kidding, in *all five* of those fields.

Impossible to relinquish your temperament. Trying to relinquish your temperament is probably like trying to relinquish your shadow.

Put That in Your Pipe
and Smoke It

One afternoon in Joppa, in a house by the sea, Simon Peter was getting hungry, and as his meal was being cooked, he fell asleep and dreamed that a big sheet was coming down from heaven, loaded with animals. "It contained all kinds of four-footed animals, as well as reptiles and birds. Then a voice told him, 'Get up, Peter. Kill and eat.' 'Surely not, Lord!' Peter replied. 'I have never eaten anything impure or unclean.' The voice spoke to him a second time, 'Do not call anything impure that God has made clean.'" As a Jew, Peter was supposed to eat only *certain kinds* of four-footed animals; *all kinds* of four-footed animals would mean ferrets and shrews and lizards and trashcan animals and other unsavory characters.

It was a dream with a message and the message

was that Gentiles were cool, too, not just Jews. If Peter really took this vision to heart and if he really has the keys to the pearly gates, then heaven has one totally lenient gatekeeper. *Come on in! Gate's wide open! Nobody's unclean, nobody's uncool!* Of course little kids already have this principle down, so they don't need to be sent Peter's dream.

One summer I took my three-year-old and five-year-old to the zoo, our principal quest being to find the zebras. However, when we finally got to the zebra habitat, as excited as my children were to see the zebras, they were equally excited to see a squirrel running around in the zebra enclosure. "A squirrel, a squirrel! A SQUIRREL! A *SQUIRREL*! MAMA DO YOU *SEE THE SQUIRREL*?"

Zebras are cool, squirrels are cool, children are promiscuously enthusiastic. They are wowed by cows, wowed by worms. Once, my little boy picked a worm out of the dirt and as it wriggled around on his hand, he yelled, loud enough for the neighbors to hear, "I CANNOT BELIEVE THIS IS HAPPENING TO ME!"

I love Peter's dream—nothing's unclean—and I try to dream it all the time and to apply it to all areas of my life, music and words and weather and moods, all areas except for the original one, the eating of animals. The other Adventist book I sold in high school, besides the answer book, was a vegetarian cookbook, and though I long ago ditched the answer book, I still like the cookbook because it leaves the animals out. Once in a while the institution

and the temperament are compatible: I'm both accidentally *and* temperamentally vegetarian. The subtraction of
meat is my favorite subtraction, and anyway one person's
subtraction can be another person's addition, like if I don't
eat *you*, you get to keep learning to play the harmonica
and watching the Perseid meteor showers come August.

How unfriendly to swallow a somebody, and animals
are somebodies, although they do have a problem with
representation. Animals are like people too: the cow's
children have big cow eyes just like my children, and animals are mothers and fathers and children and wives and
uncles and husbands—eat a goose and widow a goose,
eat a pig and orphan a pig. For me, not eating fathers or
wives or children has not been a sacrifice, because thanks
to that old busybody Ellen White, I never ate them in
the first place. Also, not offing someone means you can
tease them. It's been a good life, eating beans and razz-
ing the chickens. As Jesus said, when his disciples were
hassling him about not eating, "I have meat to eat that
ye know not of." My meat is not eating meat.

When Ellen White is on the same page as Ovid, she
can be stirring:

> The intelligence displayed by many dumb animals
> approaches so closely to human intelligence that
> it is a mystery. The animals see and hear and love
> and fear and suffer. They use their organs far more

faithfully than many human beings use theirs.
They manifest sympathy and tenderness toward
their companions in suffering. Many animals show
an affection for those who have charge of them,
far superior to the affection shown by some of the
human race. They form attachments for man which
are not broken without great suffering to them.

So Ellen White is a great prophet for you if you are
a pig. She's also a great prophet for you if you like to be
on a short, short leash, to be told exactly what to do and
not do and say and not say and think and not think and
read and not read and drink and not drink and how many
hours to wait between your graham gruel meals and to
be forbidden from ever, ever eating pickles. As bad as
getting all liquored up is getting all pickled up.

The mince pies and the pickles, which should
never find a place in any human stomach, will give
a miserable quality of blood.

The blood-making organs cannot convert spices,
mince pies, pickles, and diseased flesh-meats into
good blood.

Do not eat largely of salt; give up bottled pickles;
keep fiery spiced food out of your stomach.

In this fast age, the less exciting the food, the better. Condiments are injurious in their nature. Mustard, pepper, spices, pickles, and other things of a
like character, irritate the stomach and make the
blood feverish and impure.

For all the Adventist paranoia about the Catholics,
Ellen White is pretty popey herself. You'd think she was
sent a vision the opposite of Peter's, of a gigantic sheet
coming down from heaven with all the things that are
unclean, impure, dangerous—all the things that must be
prohibited. "We bear positive testimony against tobacco,
spirituous liquors, snuff, tea, coffee, flesh-meats, butter,
spices, rich cakes, mince pies, a large amount of salt, and
all exciting substances used as articles of food."

From the success of her institution I conclude that
there is something appealing about all this prohibition.
I bet somebody could make a pretty penny selling a chart
differentiating between right and wrong stars. *The sun
is not the only star at which it is dangerous to gaze!
Purchase our map and memorize our list of dangerous
stars, prohibited stars—the thousands of wrong stars,
whose wrongness only we can discern—stars that to look
at is blindness and imperilment to your soul.* Be careful,
be careful, be careful and blinky.

In Mr. Bliss's Mr. Miller's memoir, Mr. Miller's ancestors were said to possess "the most daring contempt of

danger." Of Ellen White, I would say that she possessed the opposite—that she possessed the most nervous deference to danger, and that out of this nervous temperament she established a whole nervous institution. I guess if you are such a nervous wreck yourself, if you really think there are so many dangerous influences out there, so many dangerous ditties and dramas and condiments and pastries and words, if you think we live on such a generally dangerous planet—she called the world a terrible influence—then it must feel imperative to keep your followers on leashes two inches long.

I happen to like exciting food, and I happen to feel that the Earth has been a good influence on me. And call me reckless but I prefer long-leash writers. Tagore has never harassed me about horseradish, Dorothy Parker has never prohibited me from sprinkling pepper on my linguine, Emerson has never forbidden me to dance the cha-cha, and Kierkegaard has never prescribed to me my thoughts. In fact, Kierkegaard *condemned* the thinking of prescribed thoughts: "People demand freedom of speech as a compensation for the freedom of thought which they seldom use."

Listening to some prophets, you'd think everything you've ever done was wrong. You've been eating the wrong condiments—vinegar and mustard!—drinking the wrong drinks—coffee and rum!—reading the wrong authors—heretics, mystics!—dating the wrong characters—boxers! bankers! cannibals!—living in the wrong neighborhood, listening to the wrong songs played in the wrong rhythm—syncopation!—on the wrong instruments—drums!—working the wrong job and attending the wrong church (always known to its adherents as "the right church"). But reading Peter's dream or watching the film *Wild Strawberries* or listening to how Miles Davis *uses* those riffs and stinkers that the other musicians throw at him makes you think, on the other hand, that the only really wrong thing is to squander experience.

Being so enthusiastically vegetarian myself, I like to translate Peter's dream into another context—from what you eat to what you smoke—and I call my version of the dream "Put that in your pipe and smoke it." To put pickles in my pipe, and whiskey, winters, stars, and weeds—even those wicked little thistles in my backyard—to smoke it all, use it all, take it all to heart, even the pains that feel like taking knives to heart.

Rather than wishing my life were easier, less wintry, less weedy, that I lived on a tropical island and had a personal enchilada chef, that I'd been born in that halcyon time before the internet but after bicycles, here's what I will wish: I wish I were alive right now with blurring vision and cracking teeth and a hardworking heart. I wish I lived in a little town in Montana, I wish the years were scrolling by, I wish my hair were turning white, I wish I had two children full of beans.

I wish I had worries, I wish I couldn't sleep, I wish I didn't have wings, so I had to walk. I wish I had grown up in an anti-pickle church, because authority that over-plays its hand is earlier apprehended, and earlier appre-hended is earlier resisted, and early resistance to blatant authority is good practice for later resistance to author-ity in its more insidious, sophisticated forms. Authority's a pathogen, but as Pasteur said on his deathbed, "The pathogen is nothing. The terrain is everything."

I wish Eve had eaten of that forbidden fruit, so we were all now exiles from ease, living out here in the danger zone, where trees fall, trucks crash, hearts stop, explanations fail—out here in this harum-scarum land where there is no gist, where nothing adds up except for minutes.

In one old Midrash, Adam and Eve get the chance to return to Eden, but then, after putzing around for a few days among the banana plants and kindly tigers, they decide to leave, hand in hand, and return to reality. How much weirder would it be for *us*, who were *born* out here—used to wresting our food out of the ground—to relocate to Eden? How incongruous would it be for us Badlanders to emigrate to Eden, that totally safe space?

I don't think living in Eden would be good for liter-ature, anyway. What kind of insipid Bible would we be reading if Adam and Eve had never eaten of the prohib-ited fruit? There's one chapter in *The Hobbit* where Bilbo and the dwarves, on their way to face down a dragon, temporarily have an easy time of it. For a couple of weeks they are well fed and well hosted by some friendly elves, but the chapter is short and the description cursory. "Now it is a strange thing, but things that are good to have and days that are good to spend are soon told about, and not much to listen to; while things that are uncomfortable, palpitating, and even gruesome, may make a good tale, and take a deal of telling anyway." Safe and easy days do *not* make a good tale, so Tolkien briskly moves on from the comfortable chapter to chapters where the dwarves get strung up in trees by giant deadly spiders, etc.

Had the hobbit never left his hobbit-hole, he wouldn't have had a story worth telling. Had the exiles from Zion never been exiled, they wouldn't have sung songs like this: "By the rivers of Babylon, there we sat down, yea, we wept, when we remembered Zion." They would have sung songs like I sang in Sabbath School when I was little. We were led through a plastic forest decorated with plastic flowers, inhabited by plastic squirrels and plastic foxes, while we sang, "Shall we go for a walk today, a walk today, a walk today? Shall we go for a walk today, to see what God has given?" Except God had *not* given us those plastic petunias or faux foxes, and facsimile forests can inspire only singsong songs.

If Ellen White received a vision opposite to Peter's, her rules were the inverse of God's in Eden: you are forbidden to eat of all the trees except the one she herself planted, her own harmless little pickle-free tree—only of that one stubby, stunted tree may you safely eat. I have nothing against abstinence; abstinence is an experience too—put *that* in your pipe and smoke it. It's just that I prefer Emily Dickinson's abstinence to Ellen White's. Here, see if you can tell which diminutive nineteenth-century New England woman wrote which lines:

> Let not one drop of wine or liquor pass your lips, for in its use is madness and woe. Pledge yourself to entire abstinence, for it is your only safety.

> *Who never wanted,—maddest joy*
> *Remains to him unknown:*
> *The banquet of abstemiousness*
> *Surpasses that of wine.*

One is abstinent for safety's sake, the other abstinent for joy. One is abstemious due to *fear* of madness, the other due to *love* of madness. The maddest joys, the wrenchingest songs, the stirringest stories—they all come from wanting. More intoxicating than *having* a thing is *wanting* it. As my meat is not eating meat, so sometimes my wine is not drinking wine, for wanting surpasses wine, and the hungriest dreams are the deepest dreams.

They manifest sympathy and tenderness toward their companions in suffering. The reason I can eat pickles with a clear conscience is that pickles do not manifest sympathy or tenderness toward their companions. Whether or not they *feel* tenderness toward their fellow pickles, I can't be certain, but they do not *manifest* it.

Eden, that safe space. I know a child who is kept so safe that I call it dangerously safe.

Representation. Some efforts at animal representation seem to me misguided: for example, the moose and bear heads I see mounted on the wall at the sporting goods store. If I were concerned with hamster representation, I would not mount hamster heads on my wall.

Abstinence. Some early Christians considered abstinence a heresy. Here is a sentence from a letter written by Basil the Great—not to be confused with Parsley the Great—"Their heresy is, as it were, an offshoot of the Marcionites, abominating, as they do, marriage, refusing wine, and calling God's creature polluted."

Wanting is more intoxicating than having. As Robert Schumann wrote to Klara Wieck, "I have discovered that nothing lends wings to the imagination so much as suspense and longing for something, as happened again in the last few days when, waiting for your letter, I composed whole volumes—strange, crazy, even cheerful stuff."

Wanting is more intoxicating than having. You know how it is—all night the longing for the sun, all day the longing for the stars.

Exempt

To a child, adults seem so knowy and facty that they must know the past and the future as well as how many teaspoons make up a tablespoon, the provenance of petunias, and the Latin name for "gorilla": *Gorilla gorilla gorilla*. Many Adventist adults (like many non-Adventist adults) pretend to know the past and the future—the provenance of the universe no less than that of petunias—and when I was little I'd have believed anything. Like, they could have told me that hippopotamuses migrate every fall from Namibia to Uruguay, sloshing across the Atlantic Ocean; that a spiral of billions of stars is called a diddly-squat; that George Washington was raised by hamsters: I'd have taken it all as gospel.

But as Rimbaud wrote, "Everything we are taught is false." Everything we're taught—not only the spurious facts but also the correct facts—is false, probably because everything we are taught is secondhand. I like to combine Rimbaud's statement with what Jim Harrison said: "The solstice says 'everything on earth is True.'" Everything we are taught is false but everything on Earth is true. Hamster facts are false but hamsters are true, and I was raised partially by hamsters and partially by my mother, who did *not* chart out the future, and partially by my father, who mowed paths into the woods behind our house, so into the woods I went, where I got raised partially by oak trees.

The trees *impartially* hosted us squirrels and greenbriers and children and mockingbirds and grapevines. The grapevines looping down from the branches were sturdy enough to swing on; the fallen oak leaves were crunchy enough to step on; the peppergrass was spicy enough to chew on; the milkweeds were caterpillary; the smell was green, even in winter; and now and then monarchs would migrate through and butterfly the forest. Monarchs are like stained glass but more dipsy-doodle. You might not think such a beautiful place could be beautified further, but it was: it was beautified by butterflies.

* * *

Sometimes Shakespeare's characters start out in cities, where there are leaders and laws and busybodies and lots of interference (marry *him*, not *him*), but in a later act they flee into the forest, where they are exempt from all the fuss, all the governance.

And this our life, exempt from public haunt,
Finds tongues in trees, books in the running brooks,
Sermons in stones, and good in everything.

In the forest one is exempt from instruction and dogma, though not from sermons, for the birds preach: *Sing.* The grapevines preach: *Climb a tree.* The lichens preach: *Patience.* The briars preach: *Your hair will grow and grow; all you have to do is don't cut it.*

St. Teresa of Ávila wrote about an "interior castle" with multitudinous rooms to discover within one's soul, but I prefer to think about an "interior Texas," with interior greenbriers tangling over everything and interior primroses popping up, pale and transient, and interior armadillos waddling through, and interior bats flittering erratically come dark, and interior warm, muddy rivers with dinosaur footprints on the bottom, as well as an interior tornado season. An interior castle might require sweeping and dusting and spoon polishing and might be static, seasonless, fully explorable, but an interior Texas would be more like Heraclitus's description of the soul:

The soul is undiscovered,
though explored forever
to a depth beyond report.

I don't usually care for categories and classifications and genres, but I do distinguish between indoor music and outdoor music, indoor books and outdoor books. Some music brings to mind castles, churches, chambers where reputations are made and tiddlywinks are played. Some music brings mountains to mind, and linns and linnets and leiothrixes and those carnelian-red rock formations down in Utah. With books it's not so much the *subject* but the *breadth*: although she writes about sitting rooms and society events, I think of Edith Wharton as an outdoor writer, since she seems to have bounced her ideas off the stars.

* * *

Along with indoor art and outdoor art there is an indoor god and an outdoor god. The indoor god is a governessy god: tidy, tame, domesticated, controlling, concerned with custom, propriety, prohibitions, with not eating nachos, not reading Nietzsche, not painting your fingernails; and Jesus is a little connect-the-dots figure in your Sabbath school magazine. The outdoor god is more like the figure you'd see if you connected the monarchs dipsy-doodling through the forest on their way to Mexico.

When I was ten I had two indoor hamsters, a blonde named Gertrude and a brunette named Ramona. When Gertrude was perched on top of their metal exercise wheel, Ramona would hop inside and run as fast as she could to catapult Gertrude across the cage, where she'd thump against the glass wall. They bickered, they brawled; their togetherness was forced upon them, though nobody forced them to sleep smushed together all day. My mother let me stay home from school the day Gertrude was sick and dying grotesquely. With their conspicuous mortality my hamsters showed me more about the future than all the prophecy cranks at church: that someday I would have four minutes of future left, three minutes, two minutes, one minute.

Even mortaller were the several orphaned sparrows my neighbors brought me to take care of. Jesus and Mahalia Jackson said God's eye is on the sparrow, but *my* eye was on the sparrow, too, but they never flourished in my shoebox. They would not be boxed, they would not be domesticated. Also mortal was a tree I gave my mother. Many people hate mesquites for their trashy habits, for how they scatter their pods all over the place, but my mother is not many people. Wanting to give her a mesquite for her fiftieth birthday, I found a tiny one growing in a field, dug and dug and dug, never got to the bottom of the root, severed it, presented the scraggly stick to her at a fancy party. It did not survive the severing, the partying, etc.

* * *

I'm no mesquite, I'm no sparrow, but I hope they rubbed off on me, with their untamability. I'm no skunk but I hope I've rubbed shoulders often enough with skunks and scorpions and squirrels and dewberries and blue-bonnets and roadrunners and armadillos and jackrabbits and monarchs and mimosas and muddy meandering rivers—enough to have an interior Texas, an inner outside, to have an outdoor heart, to carry an exemption in my heart, to be exempt from the small-time quibbles of the secondhand god. I hope that my sphere is not the spoon drawer, not the shoebox, not the cage, not the castle, and not the safe plastic forest of the Sabbath School room; I hope that, like a butterfly, my sphere is the Earth.

Interior tornadoes. Isn't it funny how the tornado is always the antagonist, never the protagonist?

The smell was green. Montana smells piney and is preposterously beautiful, but Texas got inside while I was still so permeable. (There's the apple you eat and the apple you admire.) "My heart's in the Highlands," wrote Robert Burns, "my heart is not here," but now that my body's in the highlands, sometimes my heart's in the lowlands.

Indoor hamsters. I wonder if Gertrude and Ramona were thinking, "My heart's in the desert, my heart is not here." Maybe they were not truly indoor hamsters.

Not truly indoor hamsters. Maybe indoor gods are not truly gods.

Interior greenbriers tangling over everything. If one is trying to write a coherent book, one might consult writing manuals full of organizational methods, or one might look to the forest for inspiration, where the greenbriers make everything cohere, tangling it all together with their thorny green cords. (In Montana it's the snow that ties everything together.)

I'm no skunk. And I'm no python!

Secondhand. Secondhand information can be squirrelly: I once had a churchy boyfriend inform me that God had told him I was supposed to marry him. I said, "Oh, okay," and we lived happily ever after.

Happily ever after. Not really: I said, "Sayonara!" Sayonara to annoying boyfriends and annoying churches who try to control me by speaking for God. I'll hold out for firsthand messages.

Spoon drawer. You've got your berry spoons, your sugar spoons, your salt spoons, your olive spoons, your grapefruit spoons, your egg spoons . . .

Shakespeare's characters in the forest. I have noticed that Celia, in *As You Like It*, is not talking about the internet when she says, "I like this place, / And willingly could waste my time in it."

A tree I gave my mother. I never started a forest fire but I did try to start a forest.

The figure you'd see if you connected the monarchs. What happens to that dot-to-dot figure when 84 percent of the dots disappear due to deforestation and severe weather and pesticide use, or 99 percent if you live in the West? It becomes a cruder sadder simpler fainter figure. To try and plump that figure back up, to try and alleviate the butterfly apocalypse, please reforest the earth, please remilkweed and unpesticide your yard, please have your children pray for the butterflies. (I've never been very good at praying, myself, but I do believe in the prayers of children.)

The monarchs. I'm sorry, butterflies! I'm sorry we threw you under the bus!

The March

One thing that mitigates being temperamentally at odds with your environment is your mobility. Unlike a shrub, a human can usually move to a different environment. You may feel that you do not fit in with the knitting community in Daphne, Alabama, but discover that you do fit in with the motorcycle crowd in Antler, North Dakota. You may feel out of place at a Pete Seeger tribute concert but fall in effortlessly with the Taliban. You might occasionally find yourself in environments where you fit in but where the fitting in is so vigorous that you would be scared to be somebody who did not fit in, so even though you do fit in, it creeps you out.

I had always felt like I fit in best in the forest, but when I was twenty-two, I discovered that I also fit in pretty well in La Paloma, Paraguay. After my junior year of college, I moved to the little town of La Paloma to teach community English classes, and I found myself fitting in easily, because the people of La Paloma were always late to meetings. Where everyone is late, nobody minds if everyone else is late.

During my time in Paraguay I was very happy eating *chipas* (spongy cheese buns), washing my clothes in a tub in the yard, getting to church late, and learning Spanish. Learning Spanish, I made the splendid mistakes that somebody makes when she is first learning a language. I remember once trying to say "tomato"—*tomate*—but I accidentally said *te mato*, which means "I kill you." Of course I am still learning English, but after all these years my mistakes in English are no longer as sublime as my mistakes in Spanish, French, Russian, or Greek.

But the people of La Paloma did not just show up *late* to the Free English Classes Taught by a Teacher from the United States—they did not show up *at all*. Though the rest of the world might be desperate to learn English, the residents of La Paloma were holdouts. After four months of teaching English to no one, I moved to Lima, Peru, where for a year I taught English and music to sixth graders, who were not allowed to not show up.

Nor were they allowed to show up late. In contrast to the happy tardiness I had found in Paraguay, Peru was undergoing a punctuality campaign—radio ads and TV ads and billboards all urging punctuality as the key to prosperity. I definitely felt more of a military influence in Lima than in La Paloma. The students were lined up before school every morning to have their fingernails inspected, and there was a discipline officer at my school whose job was to go from classroom to classroom whacking the unruly students with a stick.

One Sunday all the teachers and students from my school were bussed out to the countryside to participate in a march with other Seventh-day Adventist schools. We were uniformed, army-like, and army-like we were to goose-step around a circular track to military music blaring from large speakers. Now, I am not by nature much of a marcher; by nature I am more of a meanderer. Anyway, I was positioned in the ranks next to my principal, Flor Flores Ramos, which is Spanish for "Flower Flowers Branches." Because my marching was more like shuffling, Flor Flores Ramos whispered exhortations to me the whole time—"¡Los piecitos, Amycita, los piecitos!," which means "The little feet, little Amy, the little feet!," which meant that little Amy was supposed to kick her little feet higher into the air. Round and round we went, rankling each other, Flor Flores Ramos goose-stepping and whispering frantically at me, and little me dragging my little feet. This is another of those unexciting experiences, like bicycling into the wind or listening to contemporary Christian music, that feels like it is never actually over.

For the record: As a principal, Flower Flowers Branches

was very good to me, encouraging and supporting me even though I was an ineffectual teacher. I was supposed to be teaching my students how to speak English and how to play the recorder; however, when it came to language, all my students really learned was how to speak Spanish with, as they called it, an "American" accent, and can you imagine what happens when you give thirty-five plastic recorders to thirty-five eleven-year-olds? That is right: they crack one another on the head, and then they get whacked by the man with the stick.

* * *

The Peruvian countryside is not the only place where I have been made to march. When I was twelve I joined the Adventist version of Scouts, called Pathfinders, because I wanted to go camping, only to discover that our leader was a failed soldier. Having flunked out of the army somehow, he took out all his military urges on us. Mostly what we did was march around the church parking lot with Military Mike barking commands at us. He took the maneuvers of sixth graders around a church parking lot as seriously as if he were maneuvering the HMS *Hermes* and the HMS *Invincible* around the South Atlantic Ocean. Militariness is very attractive to some people, like commandy people and followy people (also servy people), but to people who just want to go camping, it is repellent.

Me, I have no military urges, only camping urges. I *have* known people, however, for whom the military life-style was redeeming. On their own they were falling apart, and the army's rules and regulations put them back together. To me, fundamentalism seems similarly redeeming, similarly regulatory, similarly military. The person who cannot regulate himself—the fall-aparty person—needs to be ruled from without, and thus he will thrive when enlisted in a rule-happy church. Adventism, with its tens of thousands of commandments, provides just such external discipline. There is no impulse, no habit, no thought, no consistency of bread, no fabric, no skirt length, no use of dairy ("Cheese should never be introduced into the human stomach"), no sport or cosmetic or condiment, regarding which Ellen White did not write a commandment. (Except for wasabi, which was out of her purview. Also Cholula.)

Now, because no one could possibly memorize her millions of niggles, they are easy to counterfeit. In Lima I knew a family where the fourteen-year-old, having been bombarded with Ellen White quotes all his life, would make up his own Ellen White quotes to sling back at his parents—"Mami, Ellen White says you should never eat while lying down!" "Papi, Ellen White says napping in the middle of the morning will make you hopelessly insane!"

One problematic thing about Ellen White is that she is dead. Having died in 1915, she is extremely dead, so we don't know what to think of anything that's come up since then. We know not to read Shakespeare, or Boethius, but what are we to think of Snoop Dogg or Chubby Checker? We know never to listen to drums, but what do we do when someone starts playing the tubax (a recently invented cross between a tuba and a saxophone)? We know the angels leave us at the door when we go into the theater to watch an Ibsen play, but do the angels ditch us when we watch a robot dancing at the mall? It is so hard to be stranded in the twenty-first century with only God as our guide.

Not by nature a marcher. When it comes to marching, my heart is just not in it. Neither are my kidneys, gonads, sinuses, earlobes, or tonsils, and my skeleton especially is not in it.

Boethius. Anicius Boethius was married to Rusticiana but he was always fooling around with Lady Philosophy. Boethius was a philanderer with philosophy. Lady Philosophy was philosophy personified, whereas Rusticiana was just a person personified. I, too, am married to a personified person, and I, too, like to consort with Lady Philosophy. I also like to gallop around on philosophy horsified, for why should personifying be the only thing we do to philosophy? Why not horsify it, moosify it, goosify it, giraffify it? I relish an early-morning swim with the fishification of philosophy.

Lima. I used to take three different buses to get to my school in Lima, and once, when I was riding a bus, the hem of my skirt went down a hole in the floor and got caught in the under-bus mechanisms, so I wasn't able to get off the bus unless I left my skirt behind. I did not take my skirt off! I can't remember how I got off the bus! How did I get off the bus? Did I not get off the bus? Am I still stuck on that bus in Lima? Is Montana just a delusion?

My mistakes in English are no longer sublime. Okay, this is not entirely true. I went into a bakery recently and tried to order "cinnamon swirl bread" but got mumbly and ordered "cinnamon squirrel bread" instead, and the woman behind the counter said, "I'm sorry?," and I accidentally asked for cinnamon squirrel bread again, and she said, "Come again?," and I ordered cinnamon squirrel bread *a third time, I'm not even joking.*

The Apicklypse

As an accidental Adventist, I grew up in the company of heterogeneous people, many of them idealistic, readerly, and generous, some with screws loose, and I was the recipient of great kindness and great steaks made of gluten. I love not eating Sister Cow and Brother Pig, and I love the Sabbath—with no commerce on the Sabbath, money gets demoted and time gets promoted. I love how I could travel through South America and Adventists always welcomed me. I was Hermanita Amycita (Little Sister Little Amy), and so many Peruvians housed me, fed me *tallarines verdes* and *papa a la huancaína*, took me exploring; one woman took me to see the floating islands of Lake Titicaca. She'd never met me but I was her little sister. It was like having relatives everywhere. (O may I be as sisterly to the stranger as they were to me.)

For all the Adventist rules and regulations, Adventist sermons can be head-spinningly unpredictable, because they're always letting amateurs preach. In Iowa City I heard a man fulminating in the pulpit against the wearing of jeans to church, and another man yelling-preaching for an hour about the university football game whose cheers we could hear from church. How dare they play football on the Sabbath. Another man preached a sublime sermon advocating for freedom of conscience. Having been spiritually dragooned himself, he knew the value of freedom. Had he not been so oppressed, maybe he would have taken freedom for granted; maybe he would have thought freedom wasn't worth a turd. (I have read some mealymouthed things about freedom by people who have never known its opposite.)

My problem is with the -*ism* more than with the -*ists*. The two most annoying things about Advent*ism*, to me, are its fetish for the apocalypse and its fear of harmless things, like coffee and cheese and dancing and bracelets and jeggings and drums and Winnie-the-Pooh (Ellen White said you're not supposed to read books where the animals talk). For the sake of concision I will call these two annoying things the Apicklypse. Of course now that I have wandered away from Adventism, I know that it is not the only place—not the only -*ism*—where the Apicklypse can be found, where some folks are fixated on the end of the world and terrified of trifles. (People are like

Adventists.) Wherever I find it, I make no concessions to the Apicklypse.

Adventism is also not the only place where popey prophets try to compel you to speak in unison, sing in unison, think in unison, march uniformly; where you are given scripts to recite and thousands of commandments to obey. Nor is it the only dogmatic movement around, but it was an excellent place to develop an aversion to dogma, to notice how instant answers to fake questions are a stunting comfort. (A fake question is a question that already has an answer.) (I like fake chicken but not fake questions, or fake plants.) I used to play the piano at a Methodist church in Illinois where any song that mentioned "fire" made one poor fellow panic and run for the back door, because his apartment building had burned down. As fire was his terrifying trigger, so is dogma mine. Dogma sends me running for the nearest exit.

Sometimes the exit can be hard to find, though—it took me thirty years to find the exit out of Seventh-day Adventism. Because you can go from the cradle to the grave within the church—getting born in Adventist hospitals, reading Adventist books and Adventist magazines, watching Adventist television channels, eating Adventist foods (fake chicken, fake bacon, fake duck, fake steak), attending Adventist schools, working in Adventist businesses, convalescing in Adventist hospitals, senescing in Adventist nursing homes—it is possible to go your whole life without receiving any outside information. In this way it is like living in a totalitarian society.

However, there is an exception to this similarity to totalitarianism, because there is a major source of outside information in Adventism: the Bible. The Bible is not an Adventist book, its truths too large, its wisdom too manifold, its questions too real. And all the Bible characters are non-Adventists, like Jesus the winebibber; like Abraham, who conversed with God directly, with no interference from an institution; like Job, insisting on the truth of his experience, controverting the dogma of his friends; like whoever wrote Psalm 115, the psalm that says you become like what you worship:

> But our God is in the heavens: he hath done
> whatsoever he hath pleased.
> Their idols are silver and gold, the work of men's
> hands.
> They have mouths, but they speak not: eyes have
> they, but they see not:
> They have ears, but they hear not: noses have they,
> but they smell not:
> They have hands, but they handle not: feet have
> they, but they walk not: neither speak they
> through their throat.
> They that make them are like unto them; so is every
> one that trusteth in them.

When you worship an unspeaking, unseeing, unhearing, unsmelling, unhandling, unwalking deity, you become unspeaking, unseeing, unhearing, unsmelling, unhandling, unwalking yourself. If you worship a miniature deity, you become miniature, too, and if you worship a dead deity, you become dead, too, and if you worship a machine, you become a machine in training. When you worship an institution, I think you lose your soul. When you worship the God in the heavens who "hath done whatsoever he hath pleased," I assume you start doing whatsoever the hell you please too.

Another element from outside Adventism is music. Good music is like honey and whiskey: it doesn't spoil—think of that Stevie Nicks song being piped into the bathroom at Walmart—and church was full of whiskey-music and honey-music. Good music carries its own priorities: beauty, vitality, intensity, soul; music can smuggle soul into the most soulless church. Steamrollers make bad musicians, as do steamrollered people—those folks flattened into the tarmac are hardly going to sweep you away with their songs. The best music in church wasn't the music with no mistakes; it wasn't the careful music but the magic music; it wasn't the ruly music but the unruly music, the music that got carried away, and the best singers sang with abandon. My favorite songs were not the marching songs but the African American spirituals that praised freedom, not obedience. "Tell old Pharaoh: /

Let my people go." "Jordan's river is chilly and cold, hallelujah. / Chills the body but not the soul, hallelujah." Hallelujah you cannot freeze my soul; hallelujah you cannot steamroller my soul.

Music is incompatible with ideology, as is experience. When I had accumulated only six years of experience, the Adventist prediction that the world would get worse and worse and worse seemed plausible. Now that I've been alive for donkey's years, I believe things get worse and then they get better and then they get worse and then they get better and then they get worse and then they get better and then they get worse and then they get better and so on.

Experience is made of strange, superfluous, elusive, uncompelled things, like a smile from a stranger; like the stripes of light, reflected from ripples on the lake, cascading down the willow trunks; like the branches sticking up out of the lake with green waterweeds stretched between their twigs so they resemble the webbed feet of dabbling ducks; like my violent desire to play the violin when I was seven. Experience is tricky, and tricky to enlist in any agenda. Not that people don't try, of course, just as they try to enlist Shakespeare. Shakespeare is like experience, tricky and wild; nevertheless, one of my professors perceived only the patriarchy in every word of *Hamlet*. (You can have a Ph.D. and still be illiterate.) Reading *Hamlet* with her felt like being suffocated: like reading the Bible with an Adventist dogmatist. Reading *Hamlet* with her felt like being trapped in a tiny stuffy stale windowless room full of dusty plastic plants, and reading *Hamlet* without her felt like getting sprung into fresh cool piney mountain air.

And so all these rogue influences—the Bible, music, experience, and possibly Lead Belly's good Lord himself: "You shall be free when the good Lord sets you free"—called to me. But in the end it was the president of Adventism himself, who, one summer Sabbath morning in 2005, showed me the exit, like a nice usher with a flashlight. I was sitting in church in Iowa City and heard the president say, in a sermon beamed out to Adventist churches all over the world, "The individual is nothing—the institution is everything." That was the moment I became a non-Adventist; that was the day I left the Institution—"I'm ceded—I've stopped being Theirs"—and joined the Individuals, like Jesus, Rahab, Job, and Abraham, and that red fox, that *real fox*, skirting the churchyard on her way to find fresh cold streams of water.

*

Not the only place. Adventism is also not the only place where one is questioned about one's ideological allegiance. In graduate school someone wanted to know what my stance was and I was stumped, I couldn't think of an answer, except for *two-legged*. But I've been thinking about the question ever since, and just now, just this morning, I finally figured out my answer: I am pro-pig, pro-petunia, and pro-hippopotamus.

"The individual is nothing." In any type of fundamentalism—religious *or* secular—the individual is nothing. Whoever you are, you are a zero, a naught, a little nobody, born only to keep its rules, obey its commands, promulgate its dogma.

I like fake chicken. I also like real chickens. This morning I saw a chicken jumping on our trampoline.

Rogues like the good Lord. Weasels are rogues too. Weasels have wills, weasels have won'ts. They are not twiddling their paws awaiting the afterlife—look at that weasel riding around on the back of a flying woodpecker.

Two of the most annoying things about Adventism. My attitude toward Adventism is admittedly skewed by my experience with the lunatic fringe, who are *really* into the apocalypse and *really* terrified of trifles. In California, Illinois, Peru, and Brownsville, Texas, I spent time with extremists and was sometimes enamored of their conviction and that is one of the most annoying things about me.

The institution is everything. Lest you think that statement was an anomaly, here is Ellen White herself talking about the General Conference, which is the Adventist government: "When the judgment of the General Conference, which is the highest authority that God has upon the earth, is exercised, private independence and private judgment must not be maintained, but be surrendered."

My Shakespeare professor. I guess she would have felt naked without her theory. A theory is like a coat. Years ago my mother-in-law gave me a long warm black coat that I wear from October through May, though one time I misplaced it for a year and felt cold and naked. Now that I am wearing it again, my mother-in-law tells me it is getting holes in it but I tell her not to say that. Anyway, Emerson urged us to "leave your theory, as Joseph his coat in the hand of the harlot, and flee."

Every word of *Hamlet*. My favorite part of *Hamlet* is every word.

PART II

✳

Consider the lilies.

—JESUS

the only Commandment I ever
obeyed—Consider the Lilies.

—EMILY DICKINSON

Old Hat

In graduate school someone asked me what I had been reading and I said Shakespeare and he said Shakespeare was old hat and I said I liked old hats. Of my eleven hats my favorite is a dumpy forest green crocheted hat I bought in Peru twenty-six years ago. Groundhogs are old hat but I like how they hog the ground and how their babies are called chucklings, and, anyway, groundhogs are new hat compared with spring. Spring is a primeval cliché—here it comes again, same old, same old sprouty old spring, trotting out its predictably green grass, its predictably purple flowers.

Lilacs are old hat, robins are old hat, cows are old hats who sometimes get turned into cowboy hats so cowboys can have a more masculine silhouette. In 1 Samuel some cows got entrusted with pulling the Chest of God to Beth Shemesh: "The cows headed straight for home, down the road to Beth Shemesh, straying neither right nor left, mooing all the way." And now, thirty-some centuries later, what are the cows doing? Still mooing all the way. The cow mooeth in the alfalfa field, she mooeth as she trudgeth down the road to another alfalfa field, she mooeth all the way to the slaughterhouse. I can hear her through the holes in the trailer.

Cows on their way to the slaughterhouse are on their way to trouble. Trouble is old hat; two thousand years ago Jesus said, "In this world you will have trouble." Trouble is an old hat I *don't* like, except in the form of babies. Babies are trouble but I don't know if they can be old hat. I was a baby once—not twice or thrice—so being a baby never got old. Maybe if I had been a baby a hundred times it would have gotten tedious. Maybe if I had had a hundred babies, some of them would have been boring babies, but I had just two and both of them were pistols.

Bambo in Italian means "silly," so *bambino* means "little silly," so *Gesù Bambino*, in that pretty Christmas song, means "Jesus Little Silly." Jesus was a little silly born on the First Noel and now I am a big silly living through the Two Thousand and Twenty-Second Noel (which would be harder to sing). Christmas is a lot of trouble—*In this world you will have Christmas*—and so I get excited not about Christmas but about the end of Christmas. At some point in my life someone took the child's heart out of my chest—*hold still*—and gave me a grown-up heart. However, I have accumulated two little sillies to whom Christmas is not old hat, whose hands I get to hold when we attend the Christmas Stroll on Main Street.

I know people, not all of them religious, who feel about the world like I feel about Christmas—they are excited not about the world but about the end of the world. Earth is a lot of trouble, long-winded like a Trollope novel, and they're ready to reach the last chapter so they can return it to the library. Not only the world but also the moon and Venus and Mercury—even the stars are old hat to them. For some people, trying to get excited about the same stars that get trotted out every night is like trying to get drunk on water. There they are again, Castor and Pollux, yawn; there's Berenice's Hair again, yawny yawn yawn.

None of the people I know who are looking forward to the end of the world are small children. Nor are they grackles or butterflies or trees. Trees are so naive, still getting drunk on water, still dancing in the wind, although once I saw—or maybe it was a dream—one tree blowing around like crazy in a row of stiff, motionless trees. It looked like feeling surrounded by unfeeling. People who are into the apocalypse are like trees who can't feel the wind; like the people in Jesus's parable who don't dance or cry when children play the flute or sing. They do not get the sads, they do not get the happies. I don't know what their problem is; it seems harder to resist children's music than to respond to it. It's like somebody removed their hearts and inserted plastic hearts instead.

* * *

In Oracle, Arizona, in the 1990s, there were trees in the Biosphere 2, living with no influences. Well, they *were* under the influence of water—but inside their geodesic dome there was no wind to topple them, no breeze to shimmy them. The protected trees didn't have any stress so they didn't grow any stress wood so they shot up fast and fell over. The Biosphere 2 trees were kept dangerously safe: before they fell down they were so feeble you could have toppled one by whispering an insult to it—*I scorn thee, scurvy tree.*

If I were a tree I'd want to be a tree on Earth, not a tree on Neptune (where the winds blow 1,200 miles per hour) or in the Biosphere 2. To a Biosphere 2 tree, the Earth is really only incidental. I want to be someone to whom the Earth is more than incidental, somebody swayable, somebody stirrable like Shakespeare, somebody responsive not only to the songs of children but also to peasantsong, prisonersong, cobblersong, queensong, donkeysong, sheepsong, somebody who, when she walks through a meadow, cannot help but dance to birdsong. It would be a shame if, in the end, the meadowlarks said to me, *We played the flute for you, and you did not dance*, and the cows lamented, *We sang a dirge, and you did not mourn*.

✴

Pollux. Pollux was a boxer. Sometimes he was a mortal boxer, sometimes an immortal boxer: Pollux toggled between mortality and immortality.

You did not mourn. I hear Keith Jarrett play "Shenandoah" and feel as melancholy as a ghost.

Dangerously safe. Growing up in the Biosphere 2 is like growing up in a church where you are protected from the wind of the Holy Spirit. The Holy Spirit, she is haywire, unpredictable, anarchic, wild like the wind. As Jesus said, "The wind blows wherever it pleases. You hear its sound, but you cannot tell where it comes from or where it is going. So it is with everyone born of the Spirit."

Influence. "Influence" comes from an old Latin word for "flow"—*fluere*. But etymology is not always definitive. "Bustard" means "slow bird" but bustards are actually fast birds who sprint across the steppes. It is as if the bonny bellflower were ugly or the common toad were rare or the Australian gecko were Zanzibari or the assassin bug were nonviolent.

Influence. I have known people who tried to influence me frying pan–style and others whose influence fluttered me like a breeze.

Slaughterhouse. Cows get trucked to the slaughterhouse so people can remove their hearts and serve them with parsley sauce.

Lucky Duck

In a letter to her brother in 1842, the eleven-year-old Emily Dickinson wrote, "The chickens grow very fast I am afraid they will be so large that you cannot perceive them with the naked Eye." Something can be so big it's invisible; for example, a chicken or a world. When I was being fitted for glasses I was told that my head was "on the small side of small." With my small-small head I have a hard time comprehending "the world," as well as "the end of the world." It is only when I think of the end of bears or bullfrogs or butterflies or rootin'-tootin' wolverines that I really start to cry.

What follows is a list of some of the characters who live in my neighborhood (or I live in theirs) who are *not* too big for me to see, whom to perceive is to adore. I might blow the world off, might even wish it away on a hard day, but I would never wish away a chickadee.

ASPEN. Sometimes the wind flutters the aspens and sometimes it flogs them, cracking their highest branches, which then hang down, their lime-green leaves turning dark brown. I tried hugging them but for years they were hanging their heads but now they have new heads.

BABY. In Bozeman there is a baby store I can't afford to shop at called the Natural Baby Company. But even though I did not buy those tiny fifty-dollar tunics and sixty-five-dollar wooden wheelie toys, the babies crawling around my yard seemed pretty natural anyway, smearing mud on their legs and munching on dandelions. What do they mean by "natural," anyhow? Is the Natural Baby being distinguished from the Unnatural Baby or the Supernatural Baby?

BEAR. If birding is watching birds then fishing is watching fish and bearing is watching bears. I bear especially in October when the bears are berrying. One afternoon a young bear climbed the neighbors' fir and everyone texted everyone. When I got the text, I was at the library and I dashed out and drove home and joined the cult at the bottom of the tree, peering up at the furry brown cult leader peering down at us. Unusually for a cult leader he was not coercive.

CHICKADEE. In the summer, chickadees are fat all day. In the winter, they are fat in the afternoon but skinny the next morning from using energy all night to stay warm. The cranes are brave to fly to Arizona for the winter and the chickadees are brave to stay here and suffer from morning skinniness.

CHICKEN. I chicken pretty frequently, for when I walk past the neighbor's house his chickens come out to greet me. They are not cagey chickens, or cash chickens, so they've been able to strike a nice balance between Possibility and Necessity. They can run out to say cluck and run back to lay their eggs.

COW. The cows are singing their hearts out, even though they are cash cows, even though they are goners. When I hear their music I think of those old lyrics that ask, "How can I keep from singing?"

CRANE. The sandhill cranes come back to Montana around my birthday, in March. Seeing them glide prehistorically into the field behind my house, and hearing them sing their prehistorically creaky songs, I am transported to prehistoric times. When they fly away in September I am restored to modern times. It is a nice rhythm, switching twice a year between the Pliocene and the twenty-first century.

DAFFODIL. My neighbor gave me some of the excess daffodil bulbs she dug up last fall (daffodils being excessive underground proliferators), and I plunked them into the ground, doubting that flowers would show up. Notwithstanding my unbelief, they showed up, but because of the spring blizzards they are hanging their heads, but still their heads are sensationally yellow.

DANDELION. Never do I doubt that the dandelions will show up.

GARDEN. My garden teaches me that you lapse only one way—into chaos. You never lapse into order. The thyme plant teaches me that it is possible to keep growing amid chaos *or* order.

GOOSE. Why do they *honk, honk, honk* when flying? Geese are such gabblers, so honky, they could honk the hind leg off a donkey.

GRASS. I didn't use to think of grass as tasty but my Pomeranian was so enthusiastic about grazing that I tried it too and discovered that grass is very sweet. Hanging out with Pomeranians is good for expanding the palate. Grass is also very pretty: today the green grass is aglitter with the melting snow.

HAMSTER. Our little pandemic hamster, cream-colored with big dark eyes, would clamp on to our hands with her razory little teeth and wouldn't let go, swinging by her teeth. She was so little; she was probably taken away from her mother too soon; she did not clench on to life as hard as she did on to our hands. When she was dying, my five-year-old, sitting on the floor in front of her cage, sobbed an impassioned speech: *Shimmer do you know that you are dying? Shimmer do you know that this is your last night on Earth? Shimmer do you know that you will never see me again?*

HAWK. It is nice to have both objective and subjective things to look at in the sky, like the objective hawk flying in front of the subjective rainbow. Rainbows are subjective, personalized—everybody sees a different one, refracted at a different angle—and the same rainbow that knocks one person down may not knock the next person down. Although once when I was driving through Bozeman there was a double rainbow that made everybody drive off the road.

JUNIPER. I like juniper berries because they remind me of gin, and I like gin because it reminds me of juniper berries. Such are the subjective joys of juniper and gin.

LABRADOODLE. Of the eight puppies in the labradoodle litter, one had straight hair, so no one wanted him, because their dream puppies had curly hair. Since we did not have a dream puppy, we took home the straight-haired doodle (who grew up to resemble a swamp creature), and now that we have him we usually want him. Except recently on a walk he sniffed out an injured deer lying under a willow, chased her across the stream and through the fire station parking lot, where she tried to hide under a van, and he bit her on the nose, and she bled, and I vowed to never let him off his leash again. I have vowed that before—to keep him on a short leash—like the time he knocked me facedown into the mud and the time he ran down the mountain to join another family. But my vows always vanish, for his penchant for freedom overpowers my penchant for control. Also it's funny to see a swamp creature hurtling up and down a mountain.

LILY. Glacier lilies act all momentary but they keep coming back every June.

MAGPIE. One afternoon we pulled out of the driveway and saw a magpie in the middle of the road. It did not move. It was stunned, having perhaps flown into a windshield, so I got out of the car and picked it up. For such a big, raven-sized bird, it was very light, and I could have thrown it high into the air, but I placed it in the backyard, and when we came back from our swimming lesson it was waiting in the fir, as if to say, *Thank you*. And then it flew away—as if to say, *Thank you, but I do not need a thrower.*

MOON. I moon, I moon, I am more momentary than the moon. But the moon is momentary, too, even if she acts all permanent.

MOOSE. I've tried moosing but moose are elusive like God. The moose reminds me of the God addressed in Rabindranath Tagore's poem: "But day passes by after day and thou art not seen." I can *think up a moose* or *research moose* on the internet, just like I can *think up a God* or *research God* on the internet, but it's not the same as an encounter. But, anyway, one time recently when I was *not* looking for a moose, one trotted by my house and I moosed unintentionally.

MOUSE. I mouse unintentionally all the time. I just found a mouse whooping it up in the corn chip bag. We have transparent orange live traps and one of us believes that the same several mice keep coming back from the golf course five miles away, where we release them, but one of us believes that although there may be a family resemblance among the trapped mice, there are enough discrepancies in tail length, eye size, ear shape, bulkiness, cuteness, etc., to confirm we are successfully relocating them.

OWL. Owling is normally more difficult than sparrowing, woodpeckering, or hummingbirding. But this spring I was able to owl from my bed, because starting at about 9:00 p.m. a great horned owl in the pine sang *oo-OOO-ooo-ooo, oo-OOO-ooo-ooo*. The other birds warbling and burbling and honking and cawing and creaking and cheeping and chirping all day were like the orchestra playing a collective prologue to the owl's solo, and I called the whole thing an Owl Concerto.

PERSON. I know there are people out there who get lost in the shuffle, like the Tokyo shuffle or the Chicago shuffle. In Chicago, most of the masses of people walking by my house were off my radar. But in Montana there's no shuffle to get lost in; almost every person who passes my house is on my radar. One elderly man in a tweed cap I think of as the Inquisitor, because if I am outside he always asks me about my denominational affiliation, and I always give a cagey answer. "What church do you belong to?" he asks, and I answer, "I am getting tired of all this snow." Another man, in a yellow-orange windbreaker, jogs by every day between 9:21 and 9:27 a.m., or did until a month ago. He used to be conspicuously present and now he is conspicuously absent.

POMERANIAN. Once, when I was walking my Pomeranian in town, a woman yelled at me, "You can't have a fox! You can't have a fox for a pet!"

PRAIRIE DOG. When you blend in with the rocks and dirt and scrub so well, and you have all those underground nurseries and bedrooms and turnaround burrows, sometimes you are secretly present and sometimes you are secretly absent.

RABBIT. One time we heard screams in the front yard and looked out and saw magpies bullying a tiny screaming bunny. We shooed the birds away, gently placed the bunny in the aspen grove out back, and she squeezed under the gate into our backyard, where my dog killed her. I buried her and did not tell the children, in whose minds she went hopping off to live a long life in the alfalfa field.

ROBIN. The robin goes yank-yank-yank and yanks most of a worm out of the ground, then bounces away and goes yanking on another worm until it's completely out of the ground, and then leaves it and bounces off, like it's not hungry but can't stop yanking. Another robin collects three, four, five worms in its beak like it can't quit collecting. Robins seem to have these compulsions, or maybe they do it for fun.

STAR. The stars in Chicago went extinct but Montana stars still shine, and I like having those sparkly intermediaries between Sunday and Monday, Monday and Tuesday, Tuesday and Wednesday.

TURNIP. It would be weird if you planted a turnip seed, and a pineapple or a pigeon showed up. But it's also weird that turnips show up, because turnip seeds are so small it doesn't seem like they'd have the atomic means for bringing forth those heavy roots and lavish greens. But—shazam—turnips turn up!

VOLE. I read somewhere that "one plus one equals two," but when it comes to voles, that's just not true. One vole plus one vole equals seven voles. I read somewhere else that "voles outwardly resemble several other small animals," and I thought it was significant that it said "outwardly" and not "inwardly," because inwardly voles may resemble gorillas.

WIND. Sometimes Montana winds approach the speed of Neptune winds. I have never seen *answers* blowing in the wind but I have seen *trampolines* blowing in winds so fierce that I wouldn't have been surprised to see *rocks* blowing around as well.

ZUCCHINI. Because I didn't have a zucchini manual and never went to zucchini school, I didn't know you have to plant at least two zucchini plants for them to actually grow zucchinis. But several summers ago I planted only one zucchini seed and the plant grew big and flowery and leafy but not fruity and thence I learned you are supposed to plant more than one, so they can pollinate each other. Failure is my school, and zucchini plants are my professors.

Well, I could go on forever but then this book would be endless and I don't know anybody who wants to read an endless book. Anyway, I fox and I phlox and I fritillary too; I pika and toadflax and speedwell and sapphire and I know a baby with sapphires for eyes and a little girl with stars for eyes and I once met a man named Reindeer and I once met a woman named Azalea. But also, sparrows squirrel and squirrels pine and robins rock, and moose goose and geese goose and chickens moon, and maybe the Jogger was jogging by my house one morning a couple of weeks ago and he jogged into the Inquisitor and was put off by his inquiries, so now he jogs along a different route.

For my part, I finally have an answer to the Inquisitor's question (you see how it takes me years and years to think of answers), so I am excited to meet up with him again. At his question my eyes will brighten and I will say, *My affiliation, sir, is not denominational! I affiliate with daffodils and doodles, turnips and babies, frickens and chogs—I mean chickens and frogs—and every once in a while I mix with a moose, and because of these affiliations I call myself not an Adventist, not a Methodist, not a Catholic, sir; rather, I call myself a member of the lucky ducks!*

The Natural Baby. To the baby store, babies are cash babies.

Donkey. "Donkey" used to rhyme with "monkey" but now it rhymes with "honky."

Owl Concerto. I've always liked how animals confuse religion, and music confuses science, and I really like how the owl, being both animal and musician, confuses both religion and science.

Animals confuse religion. As does God, confusing the religious people in the book of Job—and religious people who read the book of Job—with all his animal chatter.

Lucky duck. I am lucky I have aspens to hug—I feel sorry for you Arizonans who have to hug cactuses.

Laughing Willows

Arcturus the star—also known as Alpha Boo—is part of the Arcturus Stream, fifty-two stars moving at 275,000 miles per hour on an alternative plane to the Milky Way's. Stars get caught up in star streams like people get caught up in people streams. (I have never seen a sloth stream.) People streams can move fast too. Regarding a certain writer caught up in a political movement, Czesław Miłosz wrote, "The movement to which he was subjected went on accelerating: faster and faster, greater and greater doses of hatred and of dizziness. The shapes of the world became simpler and simpler, until at last an individual tree, an individual man, lost all importance and he found himself not among palpable things, but among political concepts."

To the accelerator, people and trees become blurs.

(The individual is nothing.) I have been an accelerator in my time, part of an apocalyptic movement accelerating exhilaratingly toward the end of time. But like stars, people can get ejected or drift away from their movement, and in my experience it's not bad to stop whizzing at thousands of miles per hour, to decelerate, to slow down enough to find yourself among palpable things rather than among concepts, to find individuals coming into focus again, to be able to see complex shapes, like the willows I drove by at forty-five miles per hour for ten years before my neighbor invited me to explore them with her.

The shape of these willows is not simple but archy and swervy and haywire. If "willowy" means "slim and lithe," then these are not willowy willows; they look like wrestlers; I think they have been wrestling the wind. They arch their trunky legs, which support dandelions and mosses and blond bugs and other pretty parasites, for example children. The children climb so high on the massive thighs that they scare themselves. (The scary height a good height to climb to in any pursuit.) (Though I suppose just to be alive is to be perched at a scary height, plummetable from.)

Downstream, some cows are wallowing under a willow extending its branches out on one side into a shady canopy. The cows have a personalized willow. The children have a personalized willow, too, for playing on; the little green worms have a personalized willow for dangling from; and the willow has some personalized caterpillars who perfectly impersonate its knotty gray twigs. I don't know if you have any personalized caterpillars but maybe you have some personalized pillows. Maybe you have a personalized puppy who dogs you, and a personalized mother who mothers you and a personalized planet that gets dark when you get sleepy and light when you wake up, with personalized plums for you to nosh on, and perhaps a personalized star, as well, who doesn't mind that you never wish upon him—everybody's always wishing on the faraway stars—but makes many of your wishes come true anyway, like the wish to stay alive, so you can bring your children to play on the willows' legs and splash in the muddy streams below, to make tenuous bridges out of fallen limbs, in those green-tinged shadows, with fluffs sparkling through the shafty light and hawks screaming at you.

I have tried to identify these willows where we willingly waste our time, but the leaves are not smooth-edged like the leaves of the peachleaf willow, nor are the twigs screwy like those of the corkscrew willow. The bark is not "shallowly fissured" like the globe willow's but deeply fissured. Nor are their branches droopy like a weeping willow's but uplifted: so I have decided to call them laughing willows. (Except one of them I call a wheely willow, since it has a rusty old wheel embedded in its trunk.) (Did a car crash into it or what?)

* * *

Children climb trees and trees climb themselves—imagine a ladder doing that. The trouble with being able to climb yourself is that you can also plummet from yourself. Along with the arching willows there is a prostrate willow that made it three or four stories into the air but then fell over in a windstorm—*whomp*. You might expect that when it fell over, the laughing willow would turn into a weeping willow. However, from its prone position, from its dead-looking trunk, little leafy fingers are sprouting up. Only the outside fell down, not the inside. "The Kingdom of God is within you." Like Walt Whitman, the tree was not contained between its hat and its boots.

The willow was only dead-*looking*, only ostensibly dead, and ostensibly dead doesn't count, like ostensibly nice doesn't count. You could be ostensibly dead for millennia and still it wouldn't count, like those microscopic worms called rotifers who were "dead" for twenty-five thousand years—stuck in the Arctic permafrost—who recently revived.

I've heard babies say "The caw is gone" and "The wid is gone" and "The poon is gone" but I've never heard them say "The thrill is gone," even when they are being force-fed mashed peas. I've heard only former babies say "The thrill is gone." But if the thrill is like the light, it's not actually gone; you've just lost your receptors for it. How dark it must seem to the fallen tree, having had such prosperity, such hundreds of thousands of leaves for absorbing light, having lost it all. But the light's still there, still streaming from the star, and as long as the tree's lost only its leaves, and not its taste for light, it can start feeling for the light again.

Some tastes are happily lost: I've lost my taste for dogma, and doughnuts; I've lost my taste for the apocalypse. I've lost my taste for vanity, for resignation. I've lost my taste for Maseratis, Bentley Mulsannes, beluga caviar, Jimmy Choos, Janus watches, Dom Pérignon, Château Cheval Blanc, and I feel lucky for the losing. Only never let me lose my taste for light, the one thing needful, the light that's still there, always there, that can be collected by the treeful, by lavish profusions of leaves, or little by little, by scraggy green shoots sprigging up out of your downfall.

Personalized planet. Some people even have a personalized god, and they give him or her a name, like Ogdy—the Siberian God—or Xwedê or Xuba or Chukwu or Lisa.

Hawks screaming at you. It appears to anger the hawks when we go over to the willows. Come on, hawks, share the troposphere.

I've lost my taste for Maseratis, Bentley Mulsannes, etc. I enjoyed those things in a past life—not the one where I was a cucumber—but am happy with my present thrift-store lifestyle.

The faraway stars. The distant stars are always begging, *Me, me, wish upon me! Hey, over here, it's Wezen, wish on me! Shut up, Wezen, look at me, ME ME ME ME, wish upon me, Prijipati!* Even Alpha Boo and Beta Boo and Mu Boo are needy-pleady, insecure, unlike the sun. I try to wish upon the sun when I think about it, since he makes most of my wishes come true, whether I wish upon him or not. It's rare to meet somebody like that who's brilliant *and* secure *and* dependable.

Little leafy fingers. If you lose your foothold, you might still get a fingerhold.

PART III

*

Sing lustily and with a good
courage. Beware of singing as if you
were half dead, or half asleep; but
lift up your voice with strength.

—"DIRECTIONS FOR SINGING,"
FROM JOHN WESLEY'S
SELECT HYMNS, 1761

Truly I tell you, unless you change
and become like little children, you
will never enter the Kingdom of
Heaven.

—JESUS

Earth Enough

I once attended a funeral where the minister trashed the dead woman the whole time. How disgusting she had been, how wicked, how sinful. If there was ever anything nice about her it was only because Jesus sometimes inhabited her body. (Jesus being so nice.) The preacher's negativity seemed to come from dogma, from theory, rather than from experience, for when the people who had actually known her (her children, her husband) talked about her, they said she was their sun and their moon. I've noticed that a lot of contemporary Christian music is similarly negative about humans, as well as about the world. Humans are yucky maggots and the singers can't wait to get rescued from this grody planet. Bands who play that kind of music in church are called praise bands, but considering their lyrics, I call them trash bands.

While Seventh-day Adventists are going to get fetched by Jesus at the end of time, after being persecuted by the Jesuits, some people in other denominations are looking forward to being swooped up *before* Armageddon. The rapture means the righteous will get to leave this unpleasant planet early, albeit naked and, some of them, toothless. They will leave their clothes and false teeth behind in little piles. From all the socks and shirts and pants on the floor in my house I might think my children had been raptured, except they are so noisy I can hear them in the basement. Also they are nothing at all like the raptured lady in *Left Behind: A Novel of the Earth's Last Days.*

In the beginning of *Left Behind*, a popular book about the rapture, a wife is already gone, having been evacuated from Earth and taken to heaven. From the descriptions of how she lived, she seems to have been primly perfect. Her righteousness was an indoor righteousness and consisted of tidiness, fastidiousness, embroidering clichés onto pillows, and opening the curtains at the same time every morning. Probably she closed them at the same time every night too. This was a woman of formidable regularity, who never gave in to a whim, never went wacko. She would have made a great employee. *Truly, I tell you, unless you change and become like predictable, clean, orderly adults, you will never enter the Kingdom of Heaven.*

And so the neatniks will ascend—*Toodle-oo!*—to enter the communion of saints, who regularly and rapturously open the curtains. Heaven must be a domestic wonderland of ruffled fabric—with weighted corners, scalloped valances, decorative tassels in coordinated shades—for the letting in of light, the shutting out of dark. *Eye hath not seen, nor ear heard, neither have entered into the heart of man, the window treatments which God hath hung for them.*

Until we can repair to the land of drapery, here we are, dusting the doodads, getting through this mandatory existence. We go on walks to humor the dogs; we blow bubbles to humor the babies; we get educations to humor the educators and haircuts to humor the haircutters. To humor the cooks we eat and to humor the humorists we laugh. They go *Joke joke joke* and we go *Ha ha ha* but we are fundamentally aloof.

But now I have *also* learned about the rapture from observing mittens. It takes one week, at most, for a new mitten to be spirited to heaven—I assume for the mittening of the saints. Those otherwise-naked curtain-saints must be wearing a lot of mismatched mittens up there. We sure are down here.

But after watching them closely—the mittens left behind— I have decided they are only superficially mismatched, that mint-colored mitten and that multicolored polka-dotted mitten both faithfully protecting the hands of a little kid sledding down the mountain backward, shrieking, whooping, with snowflakes caught in his giraffe eyelashes, plowing into a deep drift, stumbling out a laughing snowball. *Let the pious mittens go to heaven; we'll stay here with the batshit children.* The rapture of removal is not the only rapture.

* * *

Every other day Phoebe the little stuffed toy—a cylindrical tan fox with pink sparkly irises—appears to have been raptured. However, she is not pious, just losable. Luckily, she is as findable as she is losable. Her rapture consists in being lost and found and lost and found and lost again and found again, sitting on top of the piano, perching on the branch of a juniper tree, waiting in the mailbox, having been mailed to us from Texas, and, once, in the children's section of the library, hanging out with some plastic pensioners—sweater-vested, gray-haired figurines—on the deck of a pirate ship.

I am no longer capable of feeling any anxiety when we can't find Phoebe. I cannot even imagine a situation where she would not return to us. If she fell out of our backpack during snack time on a hike up the mountain, would she not wait on a boulder and then, as we passed her on our way back down, glint at us with her sparkly pink eyes? If, on a trip down the Yellowstone River, our canoe capsized and she tumbled away from us, would not an eagle mistakenly fish her out of the river and drop her down into our favorite park in Livingston, Montana? Phoebe's full name is Phoebe Finley Fluff and she deepens our sense of object permanence.

They say that object permanence—understanding that an object still exists even if it is unseen—is one of an infant's most important accomplishments. Accomplished babies can watch things come and go with equanimity, but unaccomplished babies are always spazzing out, like when the banana disappears underneath the table, like when the banana reappears from underneath the table. Babies are so shockable, so thrillable—bananas, mamas, boxes, worms—if babies had bouquets they would throw them at everything. Praise bananas, praise Mama, praise boxes, praise worms!

Maybe the day we learn object permanence is the day we start losing our penchant for praise. I once attended a concert at a suburban Chicago megachurch where the praise singers sang lengthily about having nothing to say. Contemporary Christian music seems to be good at trashing humans and bad at praising God. In chorus after verse, chorus after verse, chorus after chorus after chorus after chorus, the singers confessed that they couldn't think of any words to describe their subject. Their subject was "indescribable, indescribable . . . indescribable, indescribable." It was not clear what their subject was. "This is pallid praise," I thought. "Weird they still get gigs." I wished somebody had booked Texas Trash and the Trainwrecks instead. I sat me down weary and tried to pretend I did not understand English. If you're going to say nothing over and over, it's better to do it in a foreign language, like Old Norse: "Ek mega't hugsórr hvatvetntilr segða." (Also, between confessions of verbal destitution you could slip in some Viking mottoes.)

Why should praise be so pathetic? Were those singers just not trying? Had those young musicians ceded so soon to the void? The verbal void is a powerful—even a seductive—force. Still, I have friends who take it on daily. They are called "writers" for all the words they write, but could just as well be called "erasers" for all the words they erase. Some writer-erasers call themselves "essayists." Now, essayists like to make a big deal about how hard they try, how *essay* comes from the French word for "to try" and how, therefore, they *in particular* are tryers. Essayists are tryers for sure, but they are not the only ones—for example, I have noticed that the word *geometry* has *try* in it, too, as do *poultry*, *trumpetry*, and *ancestry*. Trumpeters are tryers, too, as are geometers and chickens and ancestors. Having recently become an ancestor myself, I am realizing how hard ancestors try.

Or was the insipidity of the praise music not a matter of effort? Were those singers not lazy but under-resourced— were their songs in fact a cry for help? Maybe some newspaper could commission a journalist to investigate the praise-music industry—all those people pressed to work in the praise-music factory with no words at their disposal, like the Children of Israel forced to make bricks without straw. Maybe if the scandal were exposed, some activists could smuggle them some material?

Because there is a lot of material out there. If you cannot muster any words yourself, you could always string together the bewitching names of South American mountains—Cotopaxi Chimborazo Illimani Illiniza Misti Alpamayo. You could transcribe the prayers of children: "Please take care of the rabbits in the snow" or "Bless the butterflies" or "Stars, don't bonk into me, moon, don't bonk into me, sun, don't bonk into me, Amen." You could even quote babies, who talk nonsense about glue and igloos, or Edward Lear, who talks nonsense about Jumblies sailing in a sieve.

You could also quote the wildlife: *Whinny whinny bleat bellow hiss buzz rattle rattle snort scream boom boom nicker boom boom*. The animals are always talking non-sense. Inspired by poets and animals and babies, you could even make up your own nonsense. Or why not quote the downpour? Why not quote the plants? I have a little girl who hears the plants whispering—she is no middling mystic—and is sometimes willing to translate: *I'm thirsty*. Those who have no plant translator and cannot think of any nonsense could always hit someone else up for words, like Robert Frost. You provide the tune, he'll supply the wit:

> *We dance round in a ring and suppose,*
> *But the Secret sits in the middle and knows.*

* * *

There was in ancient Rome a coin called a dupondius, equal in value to two asses. Although these "asses" were coins rather than donkeys, a coin *can* be worth two don-keys, and if you have the right coin you can exchange it for two donkeys, and who wouldn't rather have two donkeys than a coin? Or two tricycles or two Fudgsicles? However, there are some things for which you cannot exchange your coin. The megachurch concert showed me how money can power a flashy light show, buy giant speakers and mas-sive trucks to tour around in—but how even with the megabucks, you can't buy words. Money-poor is not the only poor. When it comes to words, "there's no purchase in money," as Shakespeare wrote. If there were, I'd spend all my money at the sentence store.

The good news, if money cannot purchase something, is that money is no object. One of the finest musical performances I ever heard required no touring trucks or laser show, no expensive equipment, not even a microphone: the singer was led to a folding chair on a little wooden stage, and he sat there and sang an old hymn. Every Saturday night at the Adventist summer camp where I worked when I was in college, there was a talent show. I'm sure the little campers told knock-knock jokes, I'm sure the preteens played the ukulele, but I have forgotten all the numbers except for one, during the session for blind campers, when a strapping blind boy with thick black hair sang this song, with gusto:

> *Brighten the corner where you are!*
> *Brighten the corner where you are!*
> *Someone far from harbor you may guide across the*
> *bar;*
> *Brighten the corner where you are!*

But, of course, songs do not *have* to have words. One could always compose just notes, like sparrows or Stravinsky.

The Rite of Spring is praise music that, rather than making people yawn, makes them riot. *The Rite of Spring* begins with a movement called "The Adoration of the Earth," wherein the Earth is tenderly, giddily, cataclysmically adored, and the bassoons sound like they are belching. Now imagine if Stravinsky had put a blank score in front of the orchestra and said, *I couldn't think of any notes for adoring the Earth.* The trumpeters would have packed up their trumpets and gone looking for a different composer, because trumpeters like to try.

Perhaps Stravinsky thought of so many notes for his praise song because he had actual subjects in mind: the Earth, the spring. Spring is a big deal for Russians. Prokofiev, after living in Paris for years, wrote, "I've got to see real winters again, and springs that burst into being from one moment to the next." Real spring is predicated on real winter, not those token winters they have in Paris. In Russia, winter keeps going long after your heart has frozen solid, but then June comes along and throws bouquets at you.

* * *

They're always telling you not to bottle up your fury, as if fury were the only thing you could bottle up. But think about the furious people bottling up all that tranquility, the mopey people bottling up their mirth, the listless people bottling up their avidity, alacrity, their fizz—will they explode óne day, like champagne? Or think of the grim people bottling up their adoration, the ones who wouldn't throw bouquets at anything. If they had a room full of bouquets, the flowers would all wither and rot.

Some people bottle up their joy better than others do. One winter when I was little my mother and I watched the Olympic figure skating competition on television. I remember one woman who skated scrupulously, perfectly, accurately—her skating was accurate to twelve decimal points. Only, she did not seem to enjoy skating, and watching her made me feel so nervous, so worried she would fall down, that I kept hiding my eyes and whimpering. She never fell but it was no fun to watch her. She was painfully perfect. Then there was another skater who fell down several times during her routine—skate-skate-*crash*, skate-skate-*splat*—except she skated with such joy that I forgot to worry about her. Her crashes were immaterial, incidental, maybe even a corollary to her exuberance. If she were a soup-maker she'd always be falling into the soup.

Hers was the trajectory of a champagne cork. Propelled by joy, she was better than perfect, and it seemed that if a great hand had reached down and removed the Olympic arena and all the crews with all their cameras and had replaced the thirteen thousand spectators with trees, with a forest of evergreens surrounding the oval of ice, she would hardly have noticed. She was a what-the-hell skater, like those teenage monkeys who fall flamboyantly out of trees, like Abraham who was always falling on his face: Abraham "fell facedown . . ." "Then Abraham fell on his face and laughed." (This was in response to God telling him he was going to have a baby at age one hundred. Babies are good jokes.)

Like other Old Testament persons, Abraham did not seem to be aware that he was in a book starring himself, or if he was aware he didn't care. He kept falling facedown, sometimes laughing, in front of his millions of spectators, rather than timorously trying to do nothing wrong. He made mistakes left and right, like handing his wife over to kings and pharaohs, telling them she was his sister; like having a baby with a substitute woman. His was not a subtractive righteousness, a careful, nervous righteousness, an anorexic righteousness. Some fundamentalists I've known were like people trying to underweigh each other—*I'm leaster; No, I'm leaster*—with the best of them tying zero to zero. Watching fundamentalists perform always makes me nervous. Maybe the authors of *Left Behind* evicted the tidy lady from the Earth / the book for *aesthetic* rather than *eschatological* reasons—the messy characters were more interesting.

Some trees droop with fruit; some trees droop without fruit. Could it be that the praise singers I heard that evening were not impaired or impoverished but practicing safe righteousness, like safe sex—a safe, barren, fruitless righteousness, in their songs that said nothing? For if you say nothing you will say nothing wrong. Maybe their speechlessness was not a malady but a goal; perhaps they were not passively resigning themselves to the void but actively embracing it—"Hail nothing full of nothing"—trying, if they were trying for anything, to subside, to recede, to gutter out like candles, to have nothing to show for their time here on Earth.

At the same service where I heard the band I'll call Lost for Words, there was a sermon about size, accompanied by a slideshow of wider and wider shots of the universe, calculated to make us feel smaller and smaller. The message was: *God's a bigwig, you're a weevil.* Because we were such pipsqueaks compared with the galaxies, we were to sit there simpering, sniveling, embarrassed to have been noticed by someone as enormous as God. However, as this fellow strenuously hyped the size of the universe, I felt embarrassed not for me but for *him* because he had so totally forgotten about amethysts and onyxes and tiny golden frogs and Jacob. Jacob might have been a lightweight compared with God, but in their wrestling match Jacob won.

I can just imagine that preacher addressing a congregation of babies, showing them slides of bigger and bigger people, from toddlers to tweens to offensive linemen, trying to take those arrogant babies down a peg or two. But babies are doughty, babies are hard to chasten. Anyway, I wish I had thought to set up a rival slideshow on the stage that night, because even if we're tiny compared with the stars, we are huge compared with the heliozoans. I would have shown the congregation slides of smaller and smaller things, from garden gnomes and Ruth Bader Ginsburg on down to fern spores, and if they had watched my show instead of the other one, they would have felt chuffed at being so big.

Abraham was human-sized but he was a *haggler*, haggling with God for the souls in Sodom. Abraham talked God into not destroying the city if he could prove there were fifty good people there, then forty-five, then forty, and finally he talked God into restraining himself if there were even ten good people living in Sodom. (Apparently there were not.) Haggling is a form of hope, and hope, if it needs to, will skip a generation or two—like even if one person is too nervous to haggle for anything, he might have a son who has a daughter who does the haggling, the hoping, that he never did.

One time, I heard Mozart's *Requiem* performed at night outdoors in downtown Chicago. There was no slideshow of the universe but the stars themselves were there. Somehow the singers did not seem dwarfed but complemented by the stars; and instead of trashing themselves they sang, "Remember, merciful Jesu, that I am the cause of your journey." As I listened, I thought that if a choir was singing like that to me, how readily I would remember them—especially if I had already made a long journey for them, past blazars and quasars and starbursts and the Sombrero Galaxy and all those voids with nary a sombrero.

Someday I am going to compose a requiem for roadkill. If William Blake was right and everything that lives is holy, then so is everything that dies, even roadkill, even bog bodies, certainly wives. As a paid church pianist, I come with the venue whenever people need a wedding or a funeral. But in seventeen years I have played for only three weddings and more than a hundred memorial services— church members seem to die more than they get married. Something I have noticed, from going to so many funerals, is that people never cannot think of anything to say about their dearly departed mother, their dearly departed wife, their dearly departed sun and moon.

Even before your wife departs, you could praise her, like Edmund Spenser celebrated his wife with "her sunshyny face." If your wife doesn't have a sunshiny face, rainy faces are pretty, too, and foggy faces, or if you don't have a wife you could praise gopher faces. My favorite faces are the changeable ones, the sunny-rainy-foggy-stormy faces, like the faces I see at the post office and the playground and in Iranian films. In Hollywood movies the faces never change, as if they were being followed around by a twelve-member team holding up reflective circles and special lighting so the face is fixed, immutable, fortified against circumstance. I hope the moon never goes to Hollywood.

* * *

Fern spores are so invisibly small that some people used to believe that the spores would confer invisibility on them if they carried them in their pockets. I wish carrying fern spores in my pockets would render me invisible, but the only way I know how to become invisible is to die, like my invisible Romanian great-grandmother. Dead people are invisibility incarnate, except for a few who become holograms or set up shop in airports.

Once, on a long layover in the airport in Minneapolis (or, as my fellow travelers called it, Appley-apolis), after getting bored of riding the train from gate to gate, filling up on Tater Tots, exhausting the indoor playground, and running up and down the many moving walkways, my children and I visited the Prince store. There he was, dead but rocking on, dancing on three screens, singing about beggars and newborns and feeling tangerine. My children still talk about "the man who died." They say, "He sang," instead of "he said," and he never sang about running out of words.

When I think about newborns or tangerines or the pretty lamb I held on a hill one time in England, it seems sad for singers to sing about nothing. Even buzzards are better than nothing, even stink bugs, not to mention monkey puzzle trees and pygmy owls and lespedezas, yams, fennel, Castelvetrano olives, sheep cheese, sopapillas, spinach—spinach is the shizzle. One could sing of high-profile things like the Pyrenees, or low-profile things like potatoes. Potatoes are perpetuators, perpetuating us as well as themselves. Or one could praise fern spores, which may or may not produce invisibility but sure enough produce ferns. When they first become visible, ferns are tiny, fuzzy, and chartreuse.

I wish I even *believed* that carrying fern spores in my pocket would make me invisible, since one's beliefs have a big influence on one's experience. What if you believed you'd be fused forever to anyone you'd wronged? What if you believed that seeing a butterfly at night meant you would die the next day? What if you really believed there was a pot of gold at the end of the rainbow? You'd drive off the road, gunning the car across the alfalfa fields to get there.

If, on the other hand, you believe there is only trash at the end of the rainbow, then there is no reason to drive off the road. Why drive recklessly to the end of the rainbow when you can just drive calmly to the landfill? Many roads lead to landfills and landfills never up and evaporate.

Where I live, the maintenance crew used to come by once a week with an old beat-up blue truck and haul our trash bags to the dumpster. But then the truck exploded, so they discontinued that service and we have to drag our trash to the dumpster ourselves. So every other week when I take my trash bin for a walk, a swarm of flies follows me. This is how I have learned that flies are fickle followers. They follow me only when I have a trash bin, whereas my children follow me everywhere I go, whether I have a trash bin or not.

If one is not acquainted with one's followers, then they have no qualities, only quantity, and one follower—fly or child, dignitary or fruitcake—is as good as any other, and the followers must have accumulated, like oodles or noodles, to be of any worth. What good is one oodle or one noodle? What good are two followers? Unless, of course, you know them. Being acquainted with all my followers, I know that most of them are flies and two of them are steadfast and true.

The problem with the contemporary star exchange— all the stars people are conferring on one another's efforts these days—is similar to the problem with followers. It is never specified what *kind* of star is being bestowed. Was that one star you gave to my easy-cheesy turnip-mash recipe a neon-rich star or a neon-poor star? You watched my instructional Autoharp video and gave it two stars, but I don't know if they were two luminous blue variables or two brown dwarfs! Luminous blue variables are blue and luminous but variable, and brown dwarfs, though constant, are very dim.

The Earth didn't get five stars—just one—but it's been star enough. That one average-sized star has been smithy enough to have forged the most original amoebas I've ever seen, and weevils unembarrassed to be weevils, and unprecedented penguins, and pansies that are pansy enough, and people who when they're not trying to halve and quarter themselves are people enough. Our sun lustily lives up to that blind boy's song, even brightening our corner vicariously, so if the scrubwoman is too busy during the day she can do her math by moonlight. For all the scrubbing, scrabbling, struggling, haggling we have to do for other things, we never have to haggle for sunlight, or moonlight.

The alien astronomer who peers across the universe at this little spiral arm of the Milky Way probably thinks, at first, that the star of our solar system is the sun. Certainly it's the flashiest, certainly the fieriest, and clearly Jupiter and Neptune are dead-end worlds. But if she looks more closely at this one world, this one little world—as farmy as Nebraska, tulippy as Holland, moosy as Siberia, jungly as the Congo; at this grassiest, mossiest, mothiest, mathiest, birdiest, berriest, airiest planet—with such a stash of consciousness, she will see that, because we have such a complementary star, the true star of our solar system is the Earth. And she will think, "How strange if it were to go unsung."

Contemporary Christian music. Because contemporary Christian music is so insipid, typos can only improve it. For example, one morning at church I saw the following words on the screen—"And we will live forever with the Lard."

No middling mystic. Sometimes this diminutive mystic puts her ear to my chest and listens to my heart and translates for me. I am lucky to have her to interpret for both my houseplants and my heart.

Tryers. In contrast to trumpeters, dulcimer players are not tryers. The words *dulcimer* and *player* have no "try" in them, just "sweet" and "play." For dulcimer players everything is sweet and easy!

The grim people. You can go around saying more and more things are not worth a gooseberry, till not even a gooseberry is worth a gooseberry—till you are aloof to the world, fit to be raptured.

Money-poor is not the only poor. As money-rich is not the only rich. *Moby-Dick* is a fortune and *King Lear* is a fortune and *Troilus and Criseyde* is a fortune: I am heir to so many fortunes.

Money-poor. Jesus didn't have much money; still doesn't. Jesus is always letting us win at Monopoly.

"Ek mega't hugsórr hvatvetntilr segða." "I can't think of anything to say."

"Hail nothing full of nothing." This is the prayer Hemingway's character prays in "A Clean, Well-Lighted Place."

"Hail nothing full of nothing." The worship of nothingness is how George Bernanos, in *The Diary of a Country Priest*, defines "essential evil": "that vast yearning for the void, for emptiness: since if ever our species is to perish it will die of boredom, of stale disgust."

"Hail nothing full of nothing." The word *naughty* comes from late Middle English and originally meant "possessing nothing." This is the real naughtiness: nothingness.

Essayists. Some essayists call themselves "nature writers" but I have a hard time understanding what this means. The word *nature* is too broad for me to comprehend with my small-small head. I *can*, however, comprehend the words *frog* and *mushroom* and *duck* and I wish nature writers would call themselves frog writers, mushroom writers, duck writers.

Dancing on three screens. Prince was raised Seventh-day Adventist but, as he said in one of his songs, he danced his life away.

Abraham a haggler, Jacob a wrestler. Those Old Testament characters were good at goosing God.

She closed them at the same time every night. I am very lazy, so I let Night close the curtains herself and I have noticed that she closes them at a different time every evening.

Jumblies sailing in a sieve. If, while you are reading poems by Edward Lear, Reason interjects—*Sailing in a sieve should have been the Jumblies' undoing*—you can suspend him. Reason is an officer and officers can be suspended.

Quantity of followers versus quality of followers. In Renaissance London, play performances for the thousands were considered rehearsals for the one: Queen Elizabeth.

Brown dwarfs invariably dim. Brown dwarf stars act like there is a moratorium on twinkling. Luminous blue variables also act like there's a moratorium on twinkling, except they are ignoring it.

The Varieties of Musical Experience

L ike those people I see at the playground and in the post office, I have a changeable face. My face is *so* changeable, in fact, that I can be incognito. When I worked at a grocery store in college, neighbors would come through my checkout line and not recognize me, week after week. Again and again the same people would be surprised that I knew them, surprised it was me, Amy, scanning their crackers and weighing their watermelons.

I am also like most people in that I have an unchangeable temperament. Except that, as a musician, I am able to *channel* other temperaments. Playing all kinds of pieces, I've been inhabited by all kinds of temperaments, all kinds of identities, like being inhabited by phantoms, lightning, mazurkas, mice. I've been vapid, treacly, giddy, bitter, sweet, rich, poor, green, blue, fervent, torpid, rowdy, niminy-piminy. I've been from Cincinnati, Winnipeg, Wyoming, Argentina; I've been a ragpicker, a floozy, a soldier, a teenybopper, a no-good fool cowboy, and an orphan on God's highway—all depending on the song. Musically I'm made of wax.

"You are the music / While the music lasts," wrote T. S. Eliot. It's true: even if normally you are a sad old square, while the "Spicy McHaggis Jig" is playing you are a young happy punk. Eliot's statement is as true as "You are the dream while the dream lasts." While the dream lasts I have a baby named Boo who never grows up; while the dream lasts the next-door neighbors have transformed their backyard into a swimming pool for dogs; while the dream lasts a herd of people is running off a cliff; while the dream lasts the fairy queen is in love with a donkey.

Playing church music has enabled me to believe some very unbelievable, dreamlike things, like one Easter Sunday in Arlington Heights, Illinois, when the band and I played "O Mary Don't You Weep, Don't You Mourn," and suddenly resurrection seemed reasonable: of *course* death gets drowned like Pharaoh's army. If, during the seven minutes we were playing that song, Ray and Billie Anne and Danny and Noni had walked into church, it would have been a surprise, yes, but a predictable surprise, like the green blades that go rising up out of their grave every spring.

Songs let you leave death, disappointment, periodontitis behind for a few minutes while they carry you away. Whitman wrote, "The orchestra whirls me wider than Uranus flies." Sometimes music whirls me to Cassiopeia and sometimes it whirls me onto my own planet—if I spend too much time in cyberspace I forget I'm on Earth, but then Woody Guthrie's songs make me say, "Earth ho!"

I'd ask my daughter, when she was a year old, to "sing a song, baby," and she'd close her eyes and sing, "La-la-la-la-la," tilting her head dreamily back and forth. I want to be like her, to abandon myself so to the song. I want to be like the lyrebird, to be possessed by a song, even if it is counter to my identity. If the lyrebird can sing koala songs and dingo songs and chainsaw songs, then I can play military music and contemporary Christian songs. At church I accompany marching songs, mousy songs, sickly songs, along with cowabunga songs. Along with songs to raise the dead there are songs to lower the living—I have often accompanied that moribund song I heard at the megachurch. That song is my gangplank and I try to walk it unflinchingly.

Of course I prefer whoopee music but one wonderful thing about contemporary Christian music is that there are no notes, no little black dots: it is all words, no dots. The best thing about contemporary Christian music is not the words (obviously) but the little letters in superscript *over* the words, denoting the chords: E—C#m—B,

repeat, repeat, repeat, repeat, repeat. Within such a repetitive sequence of E major, C-sharp minor, B major,
one may play riffs and rhythms and tangents and improvisations and countermelodies and dissonances and
never have to defer to dots, like Rachmaninoff's. That
words fail those songwriters exasperates me, but that
dots fail them makes me happy, because dots make me
nervous. Some musicians prefer dots; I prefer no-dots.
Playing dots—reading music—is like reading a script,
and playing with no dots is like talking, and talking is
like improvising: talking *is* improvising.

Dots did not fail Harry T. Burleigh, one of the first
Black American classical composers, who turned spirituals into art songs—formal performance songs for a
singer and a pianist—"Go Down, Moses" and "Deep River"
and "My Lord, What a Mornin'." If I could have met Mr.
Burleigh before he died, I would have complained about
his dots—specifically his accidentals. I would have said,
*Sir, have mercy! I can process two or three accidentals
per measure, but your songs have approximately thirty-
seven accidentals per measure! Almost every note is
sharped, unsharped, resharped, double-sharped, flat-
ted, unflatted, reflatted, double-flatted! Your music, Mr.
Burleigh, is ravishing but unplayable by all but the most
weirdly intelligent pianists.* Still I soldier on to accompany my soprano friend Mercedes. If Jesus can hear Mercedes singing Burleigh's songs, I think he is saying not

You are the salt of the earth but *You are the salt of the universe.*

Harry Burleigh also composed tunes for poems by Walt Whitman, Robert Burns, Tennyson, Christina Rossetti, and Langston Hughes, channeling each poet, each poem, letting every poem ambush him, enter him, composing a euphoric or lovesick or weary melody for it, like rejoicing with those who rejoice and weeping with those who weep. (If he had been like my Shakespeare professor he would have composed one tune and forced it onto every poem. My Shakespeare professor was unambushable.)

I wish Harry Burleigh had lived forever, so I could have complained to him about his accidentals and also so he would have had time to compose tunes for each of the 150 Psalms with their 150 variations on confidence and longing and effervescence and tears and tempests and exile and heartbreak and slimy pits and trees planted beside water. In the extremity of their variety, the Psalms resemble Emily Dickinson's poems. "Afraid! Of whom am I afraid? / Not Death—for who is He?" asks one poem in the collection, and in the very next poem the speaker winces, trembles, gasps, laughs "a crumbling Laugh," terrified to open a door:

> *I fitted to the Latch*
> *My Hand, with trembling care*
> *Lest back the awful Door should spring*
> *And leave me in the Floor—*

Emily Dickinson's temperament was capacious enough to contain so many temperaments, like the atmosphere of Earth contains so many weathers. William James could have written *The Varieties of Religious Experience* about just her.

There can be variations within variations, like how I can play "Crazy Love" by Van Morrison five times and it feels like five different songs, five different crazies; like how sometimes there's a god in the piano and sometimes there isn't. That's a variation I don't like: playing the piano without the piano god; it feels like mock music, like "music," not music. Like the god in Psalm 115, who does whatsoever he pleases, the piano god seems awfully autonomous. I want to go to a conference for musicians and I want to attend the panel where they tell you how to make the piano god stay in the strings, and also the presentation called "How to Turn Pages Without Spilling the Music All Over the Floor." For that is another problem with dots—they fall off the piano.

Of course my main objection to dots is that they are difficult. Now, up to a certain level, difficulty is propulsive; difficulty can be an invitation; most mornings Bach's *Two-Part Inventions* invite me over to the piano. However his *Three-Part Inventions* I play only in dreams in which I have three hands. On the violin I could probably make it thirty seconds into Mendelssohn's Concerto in E Minor, though screechily, and after that I would be in a pickle. If I could actually play dots I would not dislike them so much. To be able to channel Mendelssohn, Mozart, Elgar—to have those gods in your violin—must be ecstasy. I am wax but not as wax as I would be if I could play Brahms.

If I could play Brahms I might not play Amy. Why play your own dinky tune when you can channel Chopin; why write a clumsy psalm when you can read the old blazing ones; why fumble for words when you can speak Szymborska's. Why should I think my own simpleton thoughts when I could think Zhuangzi's; why attempt anything new, if it's always going to turn out so homely—these questions help me understand the fundamentalist impulse to subtract oneself, absent oneself, to submit to the script, say the secondhand things, think the pre-thought thoughts. I wish I were Schubert, I wish I were Chaucer, I wish I were my mother—

But then I remember the kingfisher impulse, more fundamental even than the fundamentalist impulse.

As kingfishers catch fire, dragonflies draw flame;
As tumbled over rim in roundy wells
Stones ring; like each tucked string tells, each hung
    bell's
Bow swung finds tongue to fling out broad its
    name;
Each mortal thing does one thing and the same:

Deals out that being indoors each one dwells;
Selves—goes itself; myself it speaks and spells,
Crying Whát I dó is me: for that I came.

According to Gerard Manley Hopkins, each mortal thing—
kingfisher, dragonfly, daughter, doctor, trucker, tiger, pagan, punk, and square—has an irrepressible impulse to
be itself. As fun as it is to channel giants and saints, I
still have this desire, unaccountable and uncontainable,
to channel myself: as much as I wish I were someone else,
more deeply do I wish I were me.

*

Sickly songs. The composer of sickly songs is a princess and the world is her pea.

I wish I were Chaucer. If it is a challenge, sometimes, to not wish I were someone else, it can also be a challenge to not wish someone *else* were someone else. Like maybe you wish the boxer were a ballerina, or Emily Dickinson were Margaret Sanger, or the thistle were a tulip. I once held a job where everybody wished I were Lance. Lance had preceded me; Lance had thrown phenomenal parties. I was a thistle; he was a tulip. The desire for me to be Lance was so general, so overwhelming, that I, too, started wishing I were Lance. The person who saved me was my dog, who never once said he wished I were Lance.

Everybody wished I were Lance. What would it be like to be Lance, to be someone everybody wants you to be?

To channel myself. As Solomon said, "Drink water from your own cistern, and running water from your own well."

Talking is improvising. Talking is riffing! Talking is jazz!

Earth ho! My father likes to talk about the day Amy discovered America, which was in March 1975, when I was born. I like to broaden the claim and say that was the day I discovered Earth. I got born—thank you, Mother—and said, "Earth ho!"

Rachmaninoff's dots. Rachmaninoff's "Vocalise" is the opposite of contemporary praise music—it's all dots, no words, and not only does the singer sing no *words* but also she sings no consonants! She just sings a vowel, any vowel she wants! It is like he wrote the song for an owl! Owls sing in vowels! Of course if Rachmaninoff had wanted to communicate an edifying message, he should have omitted the vowels and kept the consonants. T s sr t xtrplt wrds frm cnsnnts thn frm vwls.

Hail Nothing Full
of Nothing

Pigeonholes are always being disparaged. I never
hear any praise for them, only negativity, except
from pigeons. The pigeon who's had a long day
of seed-pecking and head-bobbing and feeding the little
squeakers can in the evening settle in to her comfortably
pigeon-sized hole. However, for the wigeon a pigeonhole
will never do; a wigeon in a pigeonhole is insufferably
squeezed. As pigeons need pigeonholes, so do wigeons
need wigeonholes and moles need moleholes and sea turtles need the Green Banana Hole off the coast of Florida.
"Hail nothing full of nothing!" The praiseworthy thing
about nothing is that it gives you wiggle room.

I lived in Chicago for seven years and I liked it a lot,
especially from inside an Ethiopian restaurant, or from

Indiana. From across the lake in Indiana, Chicago at sunset resembled the Holy City, rays of sunshine beaming out from behind its buildings, its traffic imperceptible. Of course Chicago *is* holy, as least as holy as Jerusalem and totally as holy as Toledo. I raptured myself from Chicago not because there were no raptures there. There were—for example, Picasso's *Old Guitarist*, and the lake, sometimes blue and sometimes gray, sometimes warm and sometimes cold, sometimes clear and sometimes opaque. Chicago is built beside one very moody lake. And there were the little mummified crocodiles, the Chicago forest to bicycle through, the Vietnamese sandwiches to eat on my birthdays.

I left because of the traffic. Once in a while I still have nightmares that I am inching angrily forward on I-90, merging angrily onto I-94, taking the 55 to the 294 and then inching back onto I-90, looping around and around on that concrete symbol for infinity, along with millions of other angry inching drivers. Sometimes in my dream, in desperation, I get out of my car and run onto the median, but the median, with its exhausted grass, does not feel like a real escape.

Nevertheless, I'm glad for my experience with Chicago gridlock because it taught me something useful about other gridlocks; for example, conversational gridlock. Some conversations have the feel of Chicago traffic, with everybody talking about the same thing, going in the same or opposite directions in a long, slow, angry, exhausted, never-ending loop. What I have learned from all my driving is that if you're headed west on I-90 and get sick of the traffic, all you have to do is *not take the 55*: if you stay on I-90 long enough, you'll end up in the Crazy Mountains. The Crazy Mountains are said to be "elusive" but the Crazies are elusive only if you do not go there.

Or you could as easily go east until you arrive in Dennis, Massachusetts, and get out of the car and go cranberrying. Or why not drive north to Manitoba and go gooseberrying? To migrate in the mind requires no Camry; you can do it even in the gulag. The good thing about being in the gulag, according to Aleksandr Solzhenitsyn, is that you no longer have to go to meetings. Instead of going to meetings you can think. As he wrote, in *The Gulag Archipelago*,

> It is a good thing *to think* in prison, but it is not bad in camp either. Because, and this is the main thing, there are no *meetings*. For ten years you are free from all kinds of meetings! Is that not mountain air? While they openly claim your labor and your body, to the point of exhaustion and even death, the camp keepers do not encroach at all on your thoughts. They do not try to screw down

your brains and to fasten them in place. And this results in a sensation of freedom of much greater magnitude than the freedom of one's feet . . .

Fulminating about meetings in the book of Isaiah, God says, "Monthly conferences, weekly Sabbaths, special meetings—meetings, meetings, meetings—I can't stand one more! Meetings for this, meetings for that. I hate them! You've worn me out!" God and Solzhenitsyn and Crazy Horse are simpatico. "For almost the whole of his life [Crazy Horse] did avoid all parleys, councils, treaty sessions, and any meeting of an administrative or political nature, not merely with whites but with his own people as well," wrote Larry McMurtry about Crazy Horse, who is being chiseled into Thunderhead Mountain in South Dakota. The chiseling has been going on for about seventy-two years now and so far he has a face. As much as he loved mountains, as much as he avoided being photographed, Crazy Horse might not appreciate a mountain being effaced with his face. But at least they are not carving three other faces cheek to cheek with him in the same mountainside, in a never-ending meeting, like they did to those dudes down the road. Also, they are going to give him his horse. Someday he will have a horse as well as a face.

I wish I had a horse as well as a face. In Shakespeare's plays people are always saying "To horse, to horse!," and

I wish I were like Malcolm or Lord Ross or Prince Henry and had a horse to back me up when I say "To horse, to horse!"—for example, when there is a meeting to attend—"To horse, to horse!"—or when the children are taking a break from being good—"To horse, to horse!"—or when a party-sized bag of salted peanuts has spilled into the deep-shag carpet.

If I had a horse I would to horse with all my heart. However, as I have no horse I am free to refer to alternative animals—"To yak, to yak!" "To emu, to emu!" "To hippopotamus, to hippopotamus!" Except I never say "To elephant, to elephant," because once, in Mexico, an elephant picked me up with her trunk, and instead of running away with me, pounding through the mahogany forests, splashing through lagoons, trundling over mountains, delivering me finally to the beach, she just stood there, dangling me by the wrist. Elephants don't abscond with you; they just dangle you in the air.

Sometimes I say "To Melville, to Melville!" or "To piano, to piano!" But I never say "To organ, to organ!" As a church organist I can produce no freedom, and even though I have been to *The School of Velocity* (a book of finger exercises by Czerny), no speed. I don't even attempt to play Bach's music on the organ anymore, because every time I tried, I looked out the window and saw him walking away, in his long blue frock coat, leaving the church premises. When I press the keys, I cannot push the stops;

when I push the stops, I cannot play the pedals; and when I am playing the pedals or pushing the stops, I cannot play the keys. Neither can I switch between the several manuals of keys without losing a measure or two. Playing the organ feels like pushing buttons, like the buttons on the dashboard of a 747 in a tailspin.

Thus petrified, and with no dynamics, I am able to sound only strident: stridently loud, stridently soft, stridently stupid. One Epiphany Sunday I thought I knew "We Three Kings" by heart, so I did not bother to bring the music (the dots) to church. But then during the service I got flustered and forgot a whole line—the line where they sing, "Field and fountain, moor and mountain, following yonder star." So instead of playing the right notes I played the wrong notes. There are five verses to that song and that particular line eluded me every time around, and I played notes that were stridently wrong.

* * *

Gabriel Fauré was a church organist away from whom Johann Sebastian Bach did not walk. Except sometimes he ran, because when Fauré was a boy, the music college he attended in Paris—the École Niedermeyer—had just one big practice room, and from the racket of fifteen boys practicing fifteen different pieces on fifteen different pianos, what composer wouldn't have run away as fast as

possible? After Fauré grew up, he played with a more reasonable number of musicians—one, an organist named
Charles-Marie Widor—and to hear Fauré and Widor improvising together on two church organs, surprising one
another with key changes, Johann Sebastian Bach must
have come loping back. (Bach, he comes and he goes.)

One piano is better than fifteen pianos, but two organs
are better than one organ, and the ideal number of instruments is, of course, three. One time I came up with this bewitching chord pattern on the piano: D—Dmaj$_7$—G—Dmaj$_7$
(repeat), A—Bm—G—Dmaj$_7$ (repeat). I played it over and
over, and a few melodies materialized and were tripping
lightly around my living room, like flappers. But after a
few days I was starting to get bored; the melodies were
starting to get languid. So I invited a clarinet player and
a flute player to come over and play my song with me
and thence so many more melodies showed up—slinky
melodies, somersaulting melodies, flamboyant melodies,
minimalist melodies who just winked. (This is the kind
of meeting I like, where everybody has an instrument.)

One April night when I was in college, a guitarist, a
mandolinist, and I climbed onto the dorm roof with our
instruments, and for several hours we invented music
under the stars. Where it was pretty it was triply pretty
and where it was sad it was triply sad, and all of it was
triply new and triply ephemeral. "You are the music /
While the music lasts," said Eliot. Now, if you play music

that's written down—like a mazurka by Scriabin, you can be the music over and over; you can be the mazurka as many times as you like, simply by turning back to the first page and playing it again. This is true even of Scriabin's *Impromptus*, reproducible because they are not really impromptu. However, with truly impromptu music, like our mandolin-violin-guitar music that night, Eliot's statement is piercing.

Still, I say there is something of the music that lasts, even when the music is over. A long time ago I read a novel that contained a detail so repulsive it obscured the rest of the book in my mind, and even now when I think about that novel, all I can remember is that one revolting detail. But the reverse phenomenon can happen too. One sublime detail can outshine hundreds of wretched pages, just as a few hours of winging it under the stars can transcend so many days of drudgery—those days that usually ensue after one has climbed down from the roof.

Effacement of mountains. Some mountains are self-effacing. Volcanic mountains like Chimborazo and Cotopaxi efface themselves.

Conversational gridlock. Of course the good thing, if everybody's discussing the same topics, is that they've got those topics *sufficiently discussed* and you are free to talk about something else. When we feel our enthusiasm for controversy flagging, it might be because we've gotten stuck on the same three or four controversies—you at your rostrum, me at mine. To reinvigorate our enthusiasm for controversy we might try reviving some forgotten controversies, like controversial Magyar rhythms, controversial methods for stringing a ukulele, or the controversial reconstruction of Janáček's *Glagolitic Mass*.

One very moody lake. Lake Michigan does not have one of those unassailable Hollywood faces.

Holy as Toledo. As I get older, I am getting holier and holier, like the celery-green T-shirt I've been wearing since 1990.

Thanks for Nothing

One day when I was in college, I walked into an auditorium and saw a woman sitting at the piano, not playing, just staring at the keys. I have thought about her over the years, the tacet pianist, and wondered if maybe she was thinking about the *Goldberg Variations* that Bach never composed. He wrote thirty variations on one little aria, variations that the accomplished pianist can play; but there are also variations on that aria that no pianist, however accomplished, can play, for they were never composed. Sometime, before you listen to Bach's composed variations, try listening to some of his uncomposed variations—in number they are infinity minus thirty. Uncomposed music is a good foil for composed music.

Other people's songs are a good foil for Bob Dylan's songs. Sometimes I'll be listening to someone's album, letting song follow song until one song comes on and I put it on repeat for the rest of the day, and when I look it up it's always a cover of a Bob Dylan song. This has happened with "Wallflower" and "Billy" and "Buckets of Rain" and "Sara" and "Tomorrow Is a Long Time" and "Boots of Spanish Leather" and "Don't Think Twice, It's All Right" and "Make You Feel My Love" and "Ring Them Bells"—so nine times. Nine times is enough to count as always.

Nothing is a good foil for something. One Saturday morning during a sermon in which the preacher had been saying nothing for at least forty-five minutes and I had surrendered to the sermon, given myself over to the void, I happened to look out the window and saw a black cat slinking by. That there was a cat out there instead of nothing was a shock I have never entirely recovered from. So I am grateful to that preacher—had his sermon been electrifying, I would never have been electrified by a cat— and to him I'd say, *Thanks for nothing!* Praise nothing: nothing sets off the cat like nothing, nothing sets off the song like silence, and nothing sets off the baby like the nonbaby.

For I've had a lot of nonbabies—babies who were never composed—and they've all been calm, quiet, and compliant, in no way like monkeys on speed. My nonbabies have never ambushed me in bed at four o'clock in the morning, jumping on my head; never clobbered one another with lemons and lint rollers; never filled my shoes with glitter; never formed a skeptical commentariat about me at the end of the hall; never walked on my yoga mat with ice skates; never, at a performance of Beethoven's Ninth Symphony, while the singers were singing "Ode to Joy," performed a corresponding "Ode to Rage"; never rampaged around the house for seven hours straight on a bouncy pink cow and a bouncy green reindeer, each toy implanted with a speaker in its head that plays loud party music. In number my nonbabies are infinity minus two.

My mother had the same number of nonbabies, and when I think about her life before my brother and I were born, I think of the trees swaying along a little road in Virginia in 1967. I have seen those red-and-orange trees in home movies from that year, from when my parents were driving down a country road and whoever had the movie camera took an unaccountably long shot of the trees along the road. There is no sound in those old movies, and though I know that trees do not sway altogether silently, still, I associate that perfect silence with my parents' lives before my brother and I arrived. When it comes to babies, forte is their forte.

Of all the loud and dangerous things in the world, I would put babies up there at the top of the list and I would say that all ancestors are brave—all ancestors are as contemptuous of danger as William Miller's ancestors, all ancestors are as brave as Dr. Danger, who routinely drives his car up a flaming ramp and crashes into a stack of buses and spends a lot of his time in the hospital. In fact, he is probably in the hospital at this very moment—*Hope you feel better soon, Dr. Danger!*

Even my ancestor whose first name was Pitiful was brave, because Pitiful had dangerous sex. All ancestors have dangerous sex: dangerous sex is not just sex where you might get diseases but also sex where you might get babies, because babies might grow up to eat pickles or join the lunatic fringe or the wrong political party—always known to its adherents as "the right political party"—or to be fractious, bumptious, peevish, yammery, and the most dangerous thing of all is that babies are desperately dear and desperately perishable. If they were only dear *or* perishable, babies wouldn't be so bad.

Still, my parents rolled out the red carpet for me. (Thus as a baby I assumed the whole world was a red carpet. Later I found out that this is not the case.) And, being the opposite of the devil, who takes violins away, my parents *gave* me a violin. When I was seven years old, a German violinmonger with a vanful of child-sized violins drove into town, and after hearing her violin propaganda, I was stricken, paralyzed with desire to play the violin. So my parents leased a quarter-sized violin for me and then a half-sized violin and later a three-quarters-sized violin and when I was thirteen they bought me the sweetest, deepest-sounding instrument in the luthier shop, and paid for hundreds of lessons over the years and drove me thirty minutes to Fort Worth and back every Thursday afternoon so I could study with a very good teacher named Joey Something.

Recently, for a course I was teaching I was encouraged to use a textbook called *Everything's an Argument*. But I decided not to use it, because I do not think that everything is an argument. Pumpkins are not arguments, porcupines are not arguments, violins are not arguments. My retort to that textbook is "No, It's Not." My argument with argument I attribute to my experience with porcupines and pumpkins and violins.

Arguments are made of words, and playing the violin has cultivated in me an obliviousness to words. Words schmords. Perhaps if that German lady had been peddling singing lessons instead of violins, I would have become a singer, trafficking in words, and would have thought of tunes as merely vehicles for far more important words— like a mule conveying fancy people around town. But if music's a mule, it's often unridable—imagine all those posh riders getting thrown off their mules, left to flounder in the dust.

Bach's fugues, for example, in *The Well-Tempered Clavier*, are not only wordless but word-proof. Trying to sing words to those four intertwining lines would sound like words typed on top of words. And some of his pieces, like the Prelude no. 3 in C-sharp major, sound like notated laughter. Next time you laugh, try laughing in words—for example Kant's words—"In whatsoever mode, or by whatsoever means, our knowledge may relate to objects, it is at least quite clear that the only manner in which it immediately relates to them is by means of an intuition." Laughter is extraverbal, antiverbal, preverbal, postverbal: my children could laugh before they could talk, and my grandmother could laugh after she couldn't talk anymore.

When Bach did compose music with words, the words were sometimes very Jewish (very Old Testament): "Be not afraid." Sometimes his words were very Roman Catholic (as in his *Mass in B-minor*) even though he was very Lutheran, and at other times his lyrics were weirdly world-weary. One time I heard a choir singing a song by Bach in praise of death. They stood in the aisles of the church and the first time through they sang in unison:

> *Come, sweet death, come, blessed rest!*
> *Come lead me to peace,*
> *For I am weary of the world.*
> *Oh come! I wait for you.*
> *Come soon and lead me.*
> *Close my eyes.*
> *Come, blessed rest!*

The second time through, they made synchronized movements with their arms to go with the words. The third time through, each member of the choir pleaded for death in her own time, in her own tempo, different from all the other members' tempos. Their gestures were no more uniform than those of the trees in the forest.

I don't usually think, "Come, sweet death," but every night I do long for oblivion. I've tried singing, "Come, sweet sleep, close my eyes, oh come! I wait for you," but sleep doesn't come any more than sheep come when I sing, "Come, sweet sheep" or sweepers when I sing, "Can anybody sweep?" Sleep is as disobliging as sweepers and sheep. In their explanations of sleep, the sleep scientists enumerate the many physical and psychological benefits we get from sleep—the memory consolidation, the muscle restoration, the hormone synthesis, etc.—and then they always say it's pretty mysterious why someone cannot sleep.

They also say it's strange that we need to sleep for *so long*. Here is a quote from the National Sleep Foundation website: "Sleep is an active period in which a lot of important processing, restoration, and strengthening occurs. Exactly how this happens and why our bodies are programmed for such a long period of slumber is still somewhat of a mystery." But I wonder if we have been asking the wrong question—why do we need *ourselves* to sleep? As wonderful as it is to be muscularly restored and hormonally synthesized, I suspect the main reason we sleep is to benefit *other people*—for example, mothers and fathers, who, after spending fourteen hours with us and our unholy hullabaloo, need a break. Maybe God, a few days after inventing us and realizing how bananas we were, invented sleep so he could sit down and put two thoughts together.

*

My grandmother could laugh after she couldn't talk anymore. Sometimes it seems like my grandmother Mimi can laugh even after having passed away, because when I laugh I feel her laughing. When Mimi laughed she'd get so carried away that her laughter turned into this desperate sort of wheeze.

Babies and nonbabies. Sometimes you hear religious people fretting about the "nones"—these "nones" being the folks who profess no religion. But compared with the difference between the person who exists and the person who does not exist, the difference between a nun and a none seems insignificant. Wimple, no wimple—who cares!

Violin propaganda. It is because of my experience with violin propaganda that I am not absolutely against propaganda. I am all for violin propaganda, bongo propaganda, panda propaganda, and also vegetable propaganda like I see on *Sesame Street*.

Your sleeping benefits other people. I don't mean to be speciesist here. Depending on your species, your sleeping might benefit *other goats, other Tasmanian devils, other koalas.*

My parents rolled out the red carpet for me. Upon being born I said, *Hello! I am not a general baby, I am a particular baby! I don't know if I'm your dream baby but I am me!* I was a little worried because dream babies are often general babies but in reply my parents said I was their dream baby. My parents are very open-minded.

Salt Is Good

Like Ellen White and the Taliban, some Catholic prefects in the nineteenth century wanted no one waltzing. In an edict sent to California in 1821, they prohibited the "*escandalosísimo* dance called the waltz." *Escandalosísimo*, in Spanish, means "really scandalous," the ending, -*ísimo*, being an intensifier—so *happyísimo* would mean "really happy" and *greenísimo* would mean "really green" and *millionísimo* would mean "really million." The other super-scandalous thing that Californians were not supposed to do was read the Bible. As Hubert Howe Bancroft wrote, "Several copies of the Bible were seen in California printed 'in common language,' a fact which caused Prefect Sarría to make zealous efforts in 1826 to prevent the reading of that book."

"If I know your sect, I anticipate your argument," wrote Ralph Waldo Emerson. I like to turn this sentence around and say: "If I can anticipate your argument, then I know you belong to a sect." This is how I know all those newspapers are sectarian and most of those books and magazines and podcasts and Twitter feeds, and how I know that Jesus was not, because I cannot anticipate his arguments. As many times as I've read his words, they surprise me every time. In the sectarian bookstore, the Adventist bookstore or Catholic bookstore or Baptist bookstore, the *escandalosísimo* Bible sticks out like a sore thumb.

The Kingdom of Heaven is like a mustard seed, which a man took and planted in his field. Though it is the smallest of all seeds, yet when it grows, it is the largest of garden plants and becomes a tree, so that the birds come and perch in its branches;

Truly I tell you, unless you change and become like little children, you will never enter the Kingdom of Heaven.

Are not five sparrows sold for two cents? Yet not one of them is forgotten before God.

But I say unto you, Love your enemies, bless them that curse you, do good to them that hate you, and pray for them which despitefully use you, and persecute you; that ye may be the children of your Father which is in heaven: for he maketh his sun to rise on the evil and on the good, and sendeth rain on the just and on the unjust.

Salt is good, but if it loses its saltiness, how can you make it salty again? Have salt among yourselves, and be at peace with each other.

What was that baby like who grew up to say "Salt is good," that little black-eyed baby squirming in the manger while a goat munched on a corner of his blanket? (There was no room at the inn for the animals either.) Unlike that megachurch preacher I heard in Chicago, Jesus did not take potshots at tiny things—salt crystals and sparrows and mustards seeds and small children—but championed them. Before I had my own small children, I did not realize how salty children are. Now I know they are *salty-ísimo*. Some children, it is true, appear to be given one teaspoon of salt for life, and in getting big they get bland and make of blandness an ideal—"Do not eat largely of salt; give up bottled pickles."

* * *

I, too, try to champion small things, like rootless duckweed. Tinier even than tiny duckweed, rootless duckweed is also known as "least duckweed." A rootless duckweed plant looks like this: o—except greener, more oval, and smaller. I admire their autonomy—they can reproduce privately, instead of having to depend on the public (birds). They need no one's help, and since duckweed floats on water, it does not helplessly wait, as other plants do, for water to drop from the sky.

Once in a while the green floating flecks might find themselves helplessly rising *into* the sky, though, borne aloft on the ascending feet of ducks, or spinning up into a tornado. But maybe when they whirl into a tornado and then drop as green specks in hail balls, or slip off a flapping duck's feet and fall into a puddle on the roof of a dime store, they meet it all with equanimity, for duckweed does not have sprigs or stalks or roots—extensions that, on other plants, get broken. You can be so small that you are unbreakable.

The smallest fish in the world is *Photocorynus spiniceps* from the Philippines, and the smallest frog is smaller than the smallest fish. It lives in leaf litter in New Guinea and is 0.3 inches long and is known as *Paedophryne amauensis—Paedophryne* meaning "child-frog." The child-frog's child is called a hopper. However small you are, your child will be even smaller (I speak from experience). The bee hummingbird, the smallest bird in the world, lays pea-sized eggs. It is also called the *zunzuncito*, Spanish for "little buzz-buzz." Little buzz-buzzes buzz around the Isle of Youth, off the coast of Cuba, intimidating the moths and frequenting the flowers and impressing the female buzz-buzzes with their iridescent red-and-blue beauty. Of course being extremely small means their beauty is extremely small, too, unlike the beauty of rhinoceroses. Also, females are not always so easy to impress, as you might have noticed. In the presence of Natty Ned or Edgy Edgar or Discussion Don, a female may feel in the mood for love or she may feel in the mood for laundry.

The Isle of Youth used to be called the Isle of Pines, before Fidel Castro renamed it, as he had promised to do: "Let's call it the Isle of Youth when the youth have done something grand with their work here . . . when they see the fruits of their labor and have revolutionized society here." If you are lazy like the pines and never get around to revolutionizing society, your island is liable to get renamed after someone else.

Castro never even considered renaming the island after *zunzuncitos*. It's not that they don't labor and it's not that their labor is fruitless; it's that the fruits of their labors are so small—those little pea-eggs, those tiny fledglings fidgeting in their cobweb nests. Also, little buzz-buzzes are difficult to lead. Leaders love the leadable, which is why they get excited about young people rather than about hummingbirds or pine trees.

* * *

I used to live in the Apartment of Mice because I have a soft, infestable heart. To the mushy-hearted, any tiny, trembly, dark-eyed creature is redoubtable. The mice in my apartment moved into my pantry, my pajama drawers, my toaster, and they nested their babies under my pillow. They walked all over me, and if they had wanted to, could have talked me into chauffeuring them around town and running into shops and buying whatever cheeses they felt like eating—mizithra, Manchego, dill Havarti, Roquefort, Tintern cheddar with chives, mimolette, Alp Blossoms, blues, and Brie. Such takeovers are no longer tolerated now that I live with intolerant people.

"Blessed are the poor in spirit: for theirs is the Kingdom of Heaven." If you are reading the beatitudes in the Gospel according to Matthew, applying them to mice might not occur to you. "Blessed are they which do hunger and thirst after righteousness: for they shall be filled." If mice can be poor in spirit, or if they hunger after righteousness, it seems like it would be hard to know. However, mice *are* good candidates for the beatitudes in Luke: "Blessed are you who are poor." "Blessed are you who are hungry." With the spiritual element subtracted, the beatitudes in Luke say simply: *Blessed are the poor, blessed are the hungry. Blessed are the wanty*, in other words. You don't have to be weighty to be wanty—just look at the mouse in your toaster.

Normal, conventional, predictable beatitudes—beatitudes that would be easy to anticipate—would say *Blessed are the influential, the prominent, the popular and successful. Blessed are ye with leverage; blessed are ye with riches; blessed are you when people like you and follow you and shower you with praise*—blessed are the havers. But Jesus lionized not the havers but the wanters. It was like lionizing mice. Actually, lions are wanty, too, so it was also like lionizing lions.

Personally I would lionize the mouse not only for being very wanty but also for being very mousy. Now, for a human to be mousy is pathetic but for a mouse to be mousy is admirable. The mousy mouse is concentrated—*mousísimo*. Actually, most animals seem *animalísimo* to me. Their vitality is the reason I wrote my first two books about them: they seem like main characters. Maybe you've looked around at family gatherings and tried to figure out who the main character was and maybe it was clearly your great-aunt Lilabeth. When I look around the world, the animals often seem to be the protagonists—even animals with the poetic rank of pigs.

The hog is whole-hog, the dog is whole-dog, the frog is whole-frog, and the bat is very batty. As Kierkegaard wrote (I am paraphrasing): The task of the self is to become itself. And animals—even the child-frogs—often seem to have achieved this task better than people, though there are exceptions, like Walt Whitman.

* * *

When I was a junior at an Adventist high school, we read Walt Whitman in a textbook designed to protect us from Walt Whitman. Before a short excerpt from "Song of Myself," a long paragraph explained how dangerous-heretical Walt Whitman was. After he was permitted, briefly, to speak for himself—"Let your soul stand cool and composed before a million universes"—there was another lengthy paragraph reiterating how pernicious he was. (Yours should not be a cool and composed soul before a million universes, but rather a wincing, sweating, discomposed, nervous soul.)

Such fortifications surrounded Emerson and Thoreau as well. However, those fortifications had the opposite of their intended effect on me. Giving me a little Whitman, a little Emerson, a little Thoreau, interspersed among all the dogma, was like giving me a little cognac in between buckets of pigswill, or little breaks from the straitjacket. Because we did not have fundamentalist textbooks for biology but rather secular textbooks, we'd tear out the first thirty pages on the first day of class, to protect ourselves from encountering evolution. We canceled evolution.

Never mind Peter's dream and never mind John Milton,

who wrote that God "uses not to captivate under a perpetual childhood of prescription, but trusts him with the gift of reason to be his own chooser." Never mind the vision God sent to St. Dionysius of Alexandria. St. Dionysius of Alexandria was a promiscuous reader in the third century—he read religious and pagan books both—until a scrupulous elder in the church found him out and shamed him.

As Milton describes Dionysius's experience in *Areopagitica*:

> A certain presbyter laid it scrupulously to his conscience, how he durst venture himself among those defiling volumes. The worthy man, loath to give offense, fell into a new debate with himself what was to be thought, when suddenly a vision sent from God (it is his own epistle that so avers it) confirmed him in these words: "Read any books whatever come to thy hands, for thou art sufficient both to judge aright and to examine each matter."

Never mind "Read any books whatever"; never mind "Thou art sufficient"—pay no attention to those super-scandalous visions sent from God. We daren't read for ourselves, reason for ourselves; we daren't venture or judge or think for ourselves. We dare not be our own choosers. Fuck those dangerous dreams from God, fuck his freedom.

After college I lived near an Adventist boarding school in Illinois that had two mottoes: "Character Above Intellect" and "Heaven Before Harvard." In other words, "Stupid for Jesus." I attended the school's church services, and in the sermons delivered there, much of what we heard was education denigrated: math and science and literature can only interfere with students' relationship with Jesus. (The question is, if I were Jesus—or even if I were myself—would I really want people following me around who would talk about nothing but their relationship with me, whose goal was to never read Wallace Stevens, never learn a diminished seventh chord on the guitar, never memorize the periodic table, never learn about rainforest monkeys—people who would only chatter on, endlessly and oafishly, about our relationship?) (Those chapel talks soured me for life on the word *relationship*.)

Leading up to graduation day at that school, the valedictorian told everybody he was going to deliver the most shocking, iconoclastic speech we had ever heard. Then, on Sunday morning, getting up to speak at the commencement service, he removed the medal hanging around his neck, threw it onto the stage floor—*clunk*—stomped on it, and kicked it down the stairs. After a dramatic pause, he announced that *that* was what his academic achievement meant to him—it was something to be vilified, violently discarded, so it wouldn't hinder his relationship (gag) with Jesus.

But I was the opposite of shocked, for he was the opposite of iconoclastic. Not an iconoclast at all—not "a person who attacks cherished beliefs"—he was, in fact, a person who cherished cherished beliefs. That young valedictorian was merely regurgitating all the indoctrination he had swallowed over the years: he was a teenager barfing up propaganda. He was a revolutionary only in his own mind—an imaginary revolutionary—and like many self-styled iconoclasts, he was really just an unwitting spokesperson for someone else's program. The pastor who delivered the commencement address that morning told us that Jesus chose James and John and Peter as disciples *because they were not educated.* (In that case, I don't know why he didn't choose chimpanzees.)

I have a different theory about why Jesus selected those particular disciples. For one thing, "The Soul selects her own Society," as Emily Dickinson wrote. For another thing, the mountain bike I bought last summer has a decal on it that reads "pedal damn it"—and to me, Jesus's disciples, including the women, seem like people who, if they'd had bicycles, would have pedaled damn it. Because when they fished, they fished all night damn it, and when they washed his feet with perfume, they spent all their money on the finest perfume they could find damn it, and when they followed Jesus, they followed him damn it even onto the surface of the water.

Those disciples were headlong—human damn it—like

the Brothers Karamazov. *Humanísimo*. Jesus said, "Let your 'Yes' be 'Yes' and your 'No,' 'No,'" but James and John and Peter and Mary and Mary Magdalene took this precept even further—their yes was a *hell yes* and their no was a *hell no*. I suspect it was their thunder, their Russianness, their *juice*—rather than their lack of education—that led Jesus to befriend them. They were like those Old Testament loose cannons; they were mortals with the dash of the mortal. Our transience is our tragedy but also our beauty, because when you don't have forever, intensity is imperative. As Solomon wrote, "Whatever your hand finds to do, do it with all your might, for in the realm of the dead, where you are going, there is neither working nor planning nor knowledge nor wisdom."

Immortals don't have the same dash, because they are not going to the grave. They have time to lollygag, to do things with a fraction of their might. They can afford to be dainty, dithering, mincing, moderate. They can putter around for decades, tread water for centuries, sit on the fence for like millennia. After hanging out with dilatory immortals for all those eons, it makes sense that while he was here Jesus wanted to hang out with people with oomph.

"You are the salt of the earth," said Jesus, "but if the salt loses its saltiness, how can it be made salty again? It is no longer good for anything, except to be thrown out and trampled underfoot." According to Jesus, *this* is what should be forcibly thrown out—not intellectual accomplishment but unsalty salt. Unsalty salt is as bad as an unducky duck, an unyammy yam, unsquashy squashes, an unfiggy fig tree, a cellist who doesn't play the cello. And when he said "Be ye perfect," I think he was telling people to be more peopley—"perfect" means "complete"—and also that he was anticipating Kierkegaard: "The task of the self is to become itself." Jesus anticipated Kierkegaard, and Kierkegaard anticipated Hopkins (with his selving kingfishers), and Hopkins anticipated Thelonious Monk: "A genius is the one most like himself."

The whole verse about being perfect goes like this: "Be ye therefore perfect, even as your Father which is in heaven is perfect." As God is very Goddy, so should humans be very humany. Perhaps this is why Jesus's first miracle was turning water into wine. Wine intensifies a person, making the Judy Judier and the Jerry Jerrier. Anyway, I find that wine makes me myselfer.

At that same conservative Adventist college in northern California (there are liberal Adventist colleges too), where I was not allowed to teach fiction, they had a different idea of perfection. They had a whole theology— Last Generation Theology—based on the idea that this is the last generation on Earth and that Jesus, although he's itching to do his Second Coming, is waiting for his followers to become perfect and sinless first, before he climbs onto his commuter cloud to float down to our planet. However, their perfection seemed a petty perfection, achieved by the avoidance of spurious sins. They seemed like a bunch of fusspots. The task of the self is to not drink coffee, the task of the self is to not read Shakespeare, the task of the self is to not wear makeup. If you wear makeup, how will Jesus recognize you when he returns?

The task of the self is to not drink wine, not eat cheese, not wear jewelry—not even wedding rings—to not listen to music with the emphasis on the second and fourth beats—that backbeat is African, and African is bad. The task of the self is to not let ladies show their knees, not let ladies wear pants, not let ladies become pastors. The task of the self is to never snack between meals. Thus could one of the saints claim he had been sinless for seven years: it's not all that hard to not snack between meals. It's also not that hard to not read Shakespeare. I see people effortlessly not reading Shakespeare all the time.

The list of sins was ever-expanding and ever-specializing, like suddenly I'd find out that not only were women not supposed to dye their gray hair brown, but also that they were not supposed to grow their gray hair long. Ye brown-haired ladies shall not bob your hair and ye gray-haired ladies shall not grow your hair long. Also fruits and vegetables must never be eaten at the same meal and the song that begins "Jeremiah was a bullfrog" is wicked, as is playing football on the Sabbath—wicked enough to inspire long loud wrathful sermons. I have never been tempted to play football on the Sabbath but I do enjoy eating an apple after a meal of vegetable potpie.

Such a burgeoning list of sins stressed me out; it felt like all of a sudden I might turn around and find that knitting the purl stitch was sinful, or standing on my head or wearing corduroy overalls or eating purple Skittles, or that doing one or the other of those things was permissible, but performing all four at once—knitting the purl stitch while standing on my head while wearing corduroy overalls and eating purple Skittles—was to hit the road to perdition. You really had to be a secretary type to keep track of all those esoteric trespasses. Blessed are the secretaries, for they shall enter the Kingdom of Heaven. Heaven will be a never-ending secretary convention.

Of course secretary types are not stressed out by proliferating prohibitions, but rather exhilarated—more items to enter into the spreadsheet! And one big advantage to coming up with new no-no's all the time—new words you mustn't say, new hairdos you mustn't sport, new songs you mustn't sing, new scoundrels to shun—is that the putzes won't be able to keep up. Leaving the putzes farther and farther behind, your purity will become ever more evident.

Personally, I aspire to be one of the putzes left behind. I aspire to be left far, far, far behind by the secretary saints—so far that I'm out of earshot, unable to hear them preaching their cheese sermons to one another. (When I lived in Paraguay I learned a saying in Guarani that meant "You go on ahead, I'll be right behind you," which was a gentler way of saying *Go away*.) As many cheese sermons as I have heard, I've never heard a great cheese sermon.

I once heard a memorable sermon about shit. The preacher asked, what if he had baked a cake that morning and brought it to church and served it to us, telling us it was 99 percent pure, that it contained only 1 percent excrement—would we want to eat it? Of course we wouldn't; we would revile it, and that is just how Jesus feels about people who are only 99 percent pure.

That preacher's recipe for righteousness was *omit the shit*. Now, my standards for cake are as high as anybody else's, but I don't believe that simply leaving the shit out makes a cake *tasty*, any more than I believe that the omission of peccadilloes makes a person righteous. If that were the case, then corpses would be the perfectest of all characters: corpses never eat pickles, corpses never snack between meals, corpses never read Shakespeare. I am more inspired by Jesus's recipe for righteousness: add salt.

My husband once had a student without any oomph.

The girl didn't do her reading, didn't do her homework, hardly came to class, but if she did she was the bareliest of there. She was pretty much defunct, a nonentity, like a seed that never sprouts. Like a corpse, she was a paragon of subtractive perfection. But in her last year, when the high school senior play came around and all the seniors had to participate because there were only nine of them, she was cast as Francis Flute in *A Midsummer Night's Dream*. She, of course, had to be pushed and prodded to learn her lines, her entrances and exits, to come to rehearsals, and during the months of practicing, her acting was nothing special.

But come opening night, dressed up as Francis Flute, she started to tell Shakespeare's jokes, and the audience started to giggle. The more they giggled, the more antic she became, till their giggles turned to screams of laughter—and then when she "died," as Francis Flute playing Thisbe, flouncing down on the stage in her ridiculous ringlets—"Adieu!"—and thrashed around and died again—"Adieu!"—the crowd whooped and cheered. I never knew that girl was dazzling until she became Francis Flute/Thisbe. After the play, I saw her sitting outside on the steps to the theater, a little sweaty, still bewigged, gazing out into the night sky, drunk on giggles. Mr. Shakespeare and Mr. Lukens had conspired to bring out a dormant girl's star power. She was salt that had lost its saltiness and was made salty again.

*

Females not always easily impressed. A female human might be impressed by Thorbium Oxmain but unimpressed by his brother Thorbium the Tardy. Hummingbirds have to deal with such female caprice too.

Buzz-buzzes are hard to lead. In response to Polonius's guidance (Polonius the would-be guider of everybody else in the play), Hamlet says, "Buzz, buzz!"

The *escandalosísimo* waltz. It's scandalous how the next generation is always waltzing in and taking over. Even when they were pea-sized, my babies took me over, body and soul. Babies are such waltzers-in.

Leaders don't get excited about pine trees. "Who can impress the forest?" asks Macbeth—as in, *Who can press the trees into service as soldiers?*—the answer to which is "No one."

"Whatever your hand finds to do, do it with all your might." One summer afternoon on the Madison River, I saw two city boys canoeing. They rowed with all their might, and had they been facing the same way, their canoe would have whooshed down the river. However, as they were facing each other, the canoe went in circles, and I praised the god of comedy.

Intensity is imperative. Solomon said there is a time to gather stones and a time to cast away stones and a time to laugh and a time to weep and a time to mourn and a time to dance (to dance!) and a time to love and a time to hate, but he never ever said there is a time to shilly-shally.

The bat is very batty. Like those little brown bats who don't stop even to drink, they just swoop over a cave puddle and take a sip and keep flying.

Secretary saints. The word *secretary* contains the word *secret* and originally meant "person entrusted with a secret." Secretary saints imagine they are in on the secret. (But no one is.)

In on the secret. Emily Dickinson wrote, "Life is the finest secret. / So long as that remains, we must all whisper."

Cheese sermons. To be fair, Ellen White wrote about other things besides cheese, pickles, and condiments. She also wrote about jokes. When you tell jokes, God doesn't like you anymore: "Lightness, jesting, and joking, can only be indulged at the expense of barrenness of soul, and the loss of the favor of God." She also rewrote the Bible, lengthily, taking all the magic out. If your problem with the Bible is that it's too magic and too short, you might enjoy Ellen White's explicated version of it.

Cheese sermons. Cheese sermons make me want to scarf down big chunks of cheddar along with hitting the hooch.

Fuck freedom. James Baldwin said most humans don't really want to be free: "I have met only a very few people . . . who had any real desire to be free. Freedom is hard to bear" and "Nothing is more unbearable, once one has it, than freedom."

The opposite of an iconoclast. The opposite of an iconoclast is a sheep. "I just wanna be a sheep, baa baa baa baa," went one of the songs we sang in Sabbath School.

Immortals can afford to be mincing. "I am too old to mince words," wrote Marilynne Robinson. But really, couldn't any of us, young or old, say, "I am too mortal to mince words"?

Blessed are the secretaries. Thank God for the organized people. The organized people help the unorganized people, whose attempt at organizing their papers goes like this: shuffle shuffle shuffle, shuffle shuffle, shuffle shuffle shuffle shuffle, I give up.

Shit cake. My Pomeranian would totally have gone for the cake that was 1 percent shit. He would have been even more excited about a cake that was 100 percent shit. Beanstan ate his own shit but still brought me so much joy that if it were up to me, I'd have him in heaven. Peace out, Beanstan.

Good Friends

I've heard a preacher (my father) say to grooms at weddings—"You may bring her great joy, or you may cause her tragic sorrow." I think this statement is true not only about brides and grooms and partners and friends, but about the world as well: "You may bring the world great joy, or you may cause her tragic sorrow." Perhaps it would be a good idea to speak this line to babies as soon as they are born. Think of the world as your friend and be a good friend to her—bring her joy, tell her jokes, plant her peach trees, compose a saxophone solo for her to play, write hilarious plays for her to perform in, dance like Prince, open up a taco bus for her, make her stained-glass windows, practice the violin eight hours a day for twenty years so you can one day perform for her the violin concerto in D minor by Jean Sibelius.

Leonidas Kavakos plays the violin concerto by Sibelius

and I feel like I am climbing around in the Tree of Life.
Some things people do make me feel like I'm in the Tree
of Knowledge, a stiff tree, whose branches are rectilin-
ear and equidistant, whose fruits are facts. The Tree of
Knowledge feels like a tree on a budget. The only birds
who'd want to be there are robot birds. But the Tree of
Life is wanton, full of sap. Birds are there singing their
heads off, bears are getting merry on the berries, the
flowers swing like paper bells. Leonidas Kavakos is a
good friend, the world was never more green.

Noah was a good friend to the world, hammering
away on the ark when he was 550 years old, smearing
it with pitch, getting it all ready to save the kangaroos
from extinction. Without Noah we'd have only the ghosts
of kangaroos hopping around now. Moses was a good
friend, leading all those captives across the Red Sea. The
paintings depict a victorious Moses marching his people
across dry land between two towering walls of seawater,
the fishies and turtles and dolphins peering curiously out
at the liberation parade. But one time I heard a rabbi say
that the Hebrew can be interpreted differently, that the
water might have been up to Moses's nose the whole time.
In retrospect the crossing was a victory but at the time it
felt like drowning.

Those medieval monks were good friends, saving all
those ancient books from extinction, so we can read so
promiscuously now. Sometimes in the margins of the

manuscripts, the scribes recorded their own feelings, such as "A curse on thee, O pen," and "Oh, my hand," and "The parchment is hairy," and "Thank God, it will soon be dark," and "St. Patrick of Armagh, deliver me from writing." Here's to those old monks, copying out Plato's works onto hairy goatskin, transcribing Aristotle and pseudo-Aristotle and hagiographies of old Serbian kings and Aelfwine's prayerbook and Albertus Magnus's treatise on falcons. The modern reader who aspires to be promiscuous like St. Dionysius of Alexandria will read not only culturally diverse books but also chronologically diverse books. How pathetic our promiscuity would be without those cursing scribes, how provincial our thinking, how reduced our unscrupulousness.

John Milton was a good friend, writing *Areopagitica*, that book with elbows that made space for other books like *Leaves of Grass* and *Emerson's Essays* and *Moby-Dick*. I've played the violin at a synagogue for the holiday called Simhat Torah, which means "rejoicing with the Torah," when everybody dances for joy because they have finished reading the Torah and they get to start over at Genesis 1: "In the beginning . . ." I celebrate my own festival called Simhat Moby-Dick when I finish the book and get to start over: "Call me Ishmael." My favorite chapter is "The Lee Shore," that call to leave the safety and comfort of the port and sail out into the open ocean. That was the chapter I read while I was in labor with my babies.

Nina Simone was a good friend, singing her singeing songs, asserting musical priorities in the world. Listening to Nina Simone and Thelonious Monk is always good for snapping me out of my practical moods. Turlough O'Carolan was a good harpist-friend; blinded at fifteen by smallpox, he became an itinerant harpist playing his pretty waltzes around Ireland in the eighteenth century, and someone transcribed them for me to play at contra dances in the twenty-first century with my friend Steve the Guitarist. During his lifetime people said that Turlough O'Carolan was too modern, but nobody says that now. (If people think you are too modern, just wait a few centuries, like Turlough O'Carolan, and if people think you are too antiquated, just wait a few centuries, like Bach.)

Bach was a good friend, writing those *Two-Part Inventions* for people to never get tired of listening to and never get tired of practicing. Like some jokes, some songs are good for only three or four listens, but Bach is the Bob Dylan of baroque composers, endlessly listenable, and his *Inventions* are egalitarian pieces, in that the left hand is no drudge, pounding out a simple rhythmic line to support the right-hand diva. The line for the left hand is as baroque as the line for the right hand. My left hand tries and fails to rise to Bach's egalitarian expectations.

We volunteers at an animal shelter in Chicago were good friends, bringing the world great joy, for the world includes dogs. To edify the inmates—to help them be more adoptable—we took them on walks and played ABBA, REO Speedwagon, Rod Stewart, and Phil Collins over the speakers and walked among the rows of fluorescently lit cages spritzing lavender scent and reading poetry out loud. Some of the dogs looked like trampled Muppets; some like pieces of plywood; and some seemed to be not just mixed-breeds but mixed-species: one gigantic pit bull named Zeus might have had hog in his pedigree.

Lydia was a black-and-white Chihuahua. The first time she was pulled from her blankets she screamed bloody murder and shivered herself nearly into a coma. Her identification microchip said she was from Mexico, but she was found wandering around Chicago in winter, a poor wayfaring Chihuahua. Her whiskers were just stubs, seared at the ends, as if she'd found a fire somewhere and got too close; her toe pads were icy and her ears were cold. Lydia needed to be warmed up, so a volunteer wrapped her in a blanket and the blanket in himself and became a human heater. The edification period ended well for Lydia—someone took a chance on her and she got adopted and adored and probably dressed in a tiny blue tea gown.

My father is a good friend. He never preaches about cheese. He says you shouldn't major in minors and that Jesus said, "Truly I tell you, whatever you did for one of the least of these brothers and sisters of mine, you did for me." He says it is more important to play four square with the lonely, clumsy kid at recess than to play with the cool kids. He says righteousness is sharing your five loaves and two fishes with hungry people and giving a cup of cold water to a thirsty person and getting down on the floor and drawing pictures with children. He says you should be like Mary pouring all that perfume on Jesus's feet, and pour your appreciation on people before they die, and he says if Adventists want everyone else to respect their consciences, then Adventists should respect other people's consciences too. He says baseball players should never be cautious when they hit the baseball, because there might be some little kid watching them for the first and last time, and they owe it to that kid to swing for the fences.

My mother is a good friend, brightening every corner she visits. If some people are like candles trying to gutter out, candles trying to never burn in the first place, candles trying to stash themselves in boxes under the bed, candles trying to bury themselves deep in the dirt, my mother is a candle burning with abandon. I have been in some damned dingy corners, but as soon as my mother showed up they were flooded with light.

My mother is generally happy: the adjective applies to everything she does. She is a happy puller of weeds, a happy doer of laundry, a happy fixer of toilets, a happy vice president of advancement at a university, a happy proposal writer for a baling-wire company, a happy driver to violin lessons, a happy maker of taco-looking cookies, a happy traveler with chickens on a train to Cuzco, a happy chatter with two-year-olds. As Robert Louis Stevenson described my mother, "A happy man or woman is a better thing to find than a five-pound note. He or she is a radiating focus of goodwill; and their entrance into a room is as though another candle had been lighted. We need not care whether they could prove the forty-seventh proposition; they do a better thing than that, they practically demonstrate the great Theorem of the Liveableness of Life." My mother is very smart and could totally prove *all* the propositions, but even better, my mommy the happy candle proves that life is livable.

(Once, she happily redecorated my bathroom, originally decorated by someone who had lined the walls halfway to the ceiling with knobbly beige plastic, and who had obviously gotten his inspiration from *Truck Stop Decor Magazine*. As my mother said, that original bathroom was "not done to the glory of God," but she took the plastic down and painted the walls pale blue to the glory of God. I did not help because I was busy being morning sick.)

My husband is a good friend, fighting fundamentalism in the English classroom. There are fundamentalists in English as well as in church—secretary saints in every sector. Thoreau wrote, "In literature it is only the wild that attracts us," but the English fundamentalists would say, *In literature it is only the grammar that attracts us*, or *In literature it is only the punctuation that attracts us*, or *In literature it is only the spelling that attracts us*. Mr. Lukens tells his students that you can write a perfectly spelled, perfectly grammatical, perfectly punctuated essay that is nevertheless a steaming pile of poo.

Emily Dickinson was a good friend and a bad speller. She wrote her badly spelled, imperishable poems in between baking all those perishable loaves of bread. Yesterday's bread is like yesterday's news, but yesterday's poems, if Emily Dickinson wrote them, are time-proof. She wrote:

> *To make a prairie it takes a clover and one bee,*
> *One clover, and a bee.*
> *And revery.*
> *The revery alone will do,*
> *If bees are few.*

See, this poem has grown even *more* timeless over the last century and a half. Now that the bees are factually growing fewer, reverie is more important than ever. She also wrote, in a letter to a friend, of "the only Commandment I ever obeyed—'Consider the Lilies.'" If you're going to choose one commandment to obey, that's a good one. Lilies are unworried about their wardrobes or their salvation, and Jesus said to be like them: "They do not labor or spin. Yet I tell you, not even Solomon in all his splendor was dressed like one of these." Emulating lilies, you will smell better than if you are emulating corpses.

Lilies are good friends to the world, being so idly beautiful. They are the counterexample to that wife over in Proverbs 31 who is a good friend but busy, busy, busy:

A wife of noble character who can find?
She is worth far more than rubies.
Her husband has full confidence in her
and lacks nothing of value.
She brings him good, not harm,
all the days of her life.
She selects wool and flax
and works with eager hands.
She is like the merchant ships,
bringing her food from afar.
She gets up while it is still night;
she provides food for her family
and portions for her female servants.
She considers a field and buys it;
out of her earnings she plants a vineyard.
She sets about her work vigorously;
her arms are strong for her tasks.
She sees that her trading is profitable,

and her lamp does not go out at night.
In her hand she holds the distaff
and grasps the spindle with her fingers.
She opens her arms to the poor
and extends her hands to the needy.

I've heard the Proverbs 31 wife being ragged on for being such an overachiever, but I bet her family didn't complain; nor did the poor and needy. I have been the beneficiary of vigorous people like her, like my grandmother and my aunt and my great-aunt and my mother and the mother of one my daughter's classmates who tirelessly lobbied the city of Bozeman to get the speed limit reduced from forty to twenty-five miles per hour on the road in front of the children's school. All I ever did about the speed limit was worry all night, but Cathy makes things happen.

There are many ways of being a good friend to the world. There's the spindle-grasping, arm-opening, food-bringing, flax-selecting, field-buying busy-type friend; and there's the lazy lily-type friend—and other types, too, like next-door-neighbor types. For three or four years there I was, hanging out all day every day, with the two personniest persons I have ever known (and I would gladly have spent a week or so with some indolent immortals). There were several times when, just as I was reaching the end of my rope, I heard a knock-knock-knock at the door, and there was my next-door neighbor, offering to watch the children so I could go on a walk.

I know a church secretary who is the bomb. If I bring my children to the church with me while I am practicing the organ, Mary abandons her secretarial duties and blows bubbles for them and feeds them cake and bounces balls with them. I also know a photographer whose public is my children. They are a public with no money and no cachet, but every week he mails them cards with his photographs on the front. Nobody sees rusted cars and broken bottles and green grasshoppers like Eric does. He has also built them a tepee and a puppet theater and periscopes so they can spy on me in the kitchen from around the corner. Then the King will say to those on His right, "Come, you who are blessed by My Father, inherit the kingdom prepared for you from the foundation of the world. *For I was two and you blew bubbles for me, I was four and you sent me photographs of grasshoppers, I was six and you made me a puppet theater out of a refrigerator box.*"

These people are to me the righteous, for I (along with Chihuahuas and children) am the world and they have brought me great joy. Because of my status as overchurched, I feel qualified to say this: there is zero correlation between religiousness and righteousness. I have known bad Adventists who were good people and good Adventists who were crumbums. I got canceled by a good

Adventist when I was five years old—I went over to play at my friend's house, but when her mother saw I had a pink plastic ring on my finger (I had gotten it at the dentist's office) she told me to leave and never come back. One of the best Adventists I've ever known—she followed Ellen White's injunctions to a fucking T—murdered her husband by slipping Temazepam into his smoothie.

I have also known good Adventists who were good bluegrass mandolinists, good preachers, good visitors of shut-ins, good protectors of clean water sources for a little mountain village in Lesotho, good prison psychiatrists, good dog-walkers, good canoe-builders, good nephrologists, good astronomers, good kindergarten teachers, good disaster-relief workers in Yemen, good garlic farmers, good birthday-cake-makers, etc. Because of my experience with both individuals and institutions, I defy the Adventist president's statement—"The individual is nothing"—and maintain the reverse. The institution is nothing; the individual is everything.

The end of my rope. One day during those end-of-the-rope years I tried putting myself in the giveaway pile but nobody gave me away.

Yesterday's news. In the newspaper yesterday, I read that the "noodle-shaped amphibians" that have just arrived in Miami are not dangerous. But for you, reading this three or four years from now, the news about the noodle-animals is old news and you're like, *Duh! tell me something I don't know!*

The English fundamentalists. As E. E. Cummings pointed out, some virtues are mutually exclusive, like you can be either a good grammarian or a good kisser but not both: someone who cares about "the syntax of things / will never wholly kiss you."

The English fundamentalists. No need to defer to the spellers! As John Berryman wrote, "Father Hopkins said the only true literary critic is Christ."

The English fundamentalists. Speaking to the Sabbath fundamentalists, who had been snooping on the disciples and had spied them picking grain to eat on the Sabbath day, Jesus said, "The Sabbath was made for man, not man for the Sabbath." Now, you might not have worried about whether the Sabbath was made for you or you were made for the Sabbath. But you *have* probably had an equivalent experience with English. The English fundamentalists will tell you that man was made for English, not English for man—so *defer*, you little nobody. Of course in their rightful roles—made for us—English and the Sabbath are sublime.

The Kingdom of God
Is Within You

Josh, who worked at my children's day care—I have no idea if he was religious or not, but he *was* righteous. He was a righteous comedian, telling the children killer jokes about owls and Jell-O and tricycles. Savannah, his fellow teacher, was a righteous rodeo rider from northern Montana. Who better than a rodeo rider and a comedian to work at a day care, her carrying three children in her arms at a time and him making them giggle? Together they crushed it and were deservedly famous in Room Three. In winter we were able to get to the day care center safely thanks to the righteous snowplow drivers who had woken up at 3:00 a.m. to clear the road for us. To every snowplow driver I say, as Gerard Manley Hopkins said to Christ, "Oh my chevalier!"

The children in day care were righteous, too, getting such a charge out of the world—such a charge out of rocks and rabbits and snakes and snow—and fulfilling Thoreau's requirements for goodness: "His goodness must not be a partial and transitory act, but a constant superfluity, which cost him nothing and of which he is unconscious. This is a charity that hides a multitude of sins." Real goodness is superfluous and unconscious, and with Thoreau, I prefer unconscious goodness—like sunshine and rain—to conscious goodness. I'd even say that conscious goodness doesn't count. When children grow up and their goodness becomes conscious and they're always reminding you of how much their goodness costs them, goodness seems like badness. People who flash their goodness at you are like people who flash their genitals at you except grosser.

The internet is full of flashers of both kinds. As Blaise Pascal described the internet in 1670,

> We are not content with the life we have in ourselves, and in our individual being; we wish to live an imaginary life in the thoughts of others, and for this purpose, strive to make a figure in the world. We labour incessantly to cherish and adorn this imaginary being, and neglect the real one; and if we possess tranquillity, or generosity, or fidelity, we are eager to make it known, that such virtues may be transferred to this creature of the imagination.

The internet is full of people living imaginary lives in the thoughts of others—it is teeming with imaginary beings. Imaginary beings used to look different from us—the sprites and brownies and nixies and sylphs. They had wings and sometimes were green or miniature or invisible. But now, on the internet, our imaginary beings look just like us and are called things like Sue Brown or Duncan Johnson—they have our names and faces but are more virtuous and less interesting than we are. Our imaginary versions of ourselves on the internet seem to me like demi-humans—demi-Duncans, semi-Sues. I wish we had left the imaginary being to the banshees, who were better at it.

All that striving to be seen—I think it hinders one's ability to see. The young Felix Mendelssohn was sent by his father around Europe, with the purpose of making a figure in the world. "I was to make my name and abilities known"—and indeed he accomplished this—he made his name and abilities known. But he seemed happiest early on, when he was "unknown," "unnoticed," "unseen," as in this letter describing a party he attended: "to see the lovely forms moving below the lovely pictures, and to glide around, tranquil and completely unknown amid the bustle and general excitement, unseen and unnoticed, seeing and noting many things—it was one of the most delightful evenings I have ever spent." Because he was unseen, he could see, and because he was unnoticed, he could notice.

In *Pride and Prejudice*, Lizzy wants to walk three miles in the mud to visit her sister Jane, who has fallen sick while visiting Mr. Bingley. Lizzy's mother tells her she mustn't go, because when she arrives she will be dirty. "'How can you be so silly,' cried her mother, 'as to think of such a thing, in all this dirt! You will not be fit to be seen when you get there.'" Lizzy's mother is like that megachurch preacher who wanted us, like vain girls with vain mothers, to worry about how we looked from the outside—*how dirty, how little, how pathetic.*

But Lizzy isn't vain, and she replies to her mother, "I shall be very fit to see Jane—which is all I want." To the mother who tells her she won't be fit to be seen, she says *but I am fit to see* and *that is all I want.* "Elizabeth continued her walk alone, crossing field after field at a quick pace, jumping over stiles and springing over puddles with impatient activity, and finding herself at last within view of the house, with weary ankles, dirty stockings, and a face glowing with the warmth of exercise."

If you are worried about being fit to be seen, you'll stay home and keep your stockings clean and you won't get to see your sister. If you want to see your sister, you have to get your stockings dirty. Being fit to be seen and being fit to see—these are incompatible things: if you are one, you aren't the other. Look at Emily Dickinson, the unseen seer. When I was young I thought it was fun to be seen, but now I think it is more fun to see. I want dirty stockings like Lizzy's, from all that springing over puddles, and I want a dirty face like Abraham's, from all that falling down laughing, and I want to be like a baby, who never worries about being fit to be seen.

Yesterday afternoon I took a walk with a two-month-old named Lou, whose mother was wheeling her along the sidewalk in her stroller. During our whole walk the baby looked up at the sky, and her mother said, "She likes distance." The baby didn't fret about being too little or too young or too inexperienced to look up into the giant Montana sky. She was cool and composed. She reminded me of Walt Whitman.

If that baby were as big as a whale, she'd be sure to impress the person who judges by megachurch metric. (Megachurches naturally being invested in gigantism.) But being whale-sized wouldn't mean she could see any farther than she can see being baby-sized. Nor would she impress the people actually worth impressing—for example, Emily Dickinson and Jesus and Solomon. Emily Dickinson said, "The Brain—is wider than the Sky," and Jesus said, "The Kingdom of God is within you," and Solomon said that God placed eternity in the human heart, that into our practical little pumper hearts was inserted eternity.

Our identity does feel ambiguous at times, like we're accidentally tiny and temperamentally huge, accidentally temporary and temperamentally eternal—trying to find our lost library books, drinking the children's tea gone cold, eating the children's bagels gone stale, fishing the peanuts out of the rug, oiling the hamster wheel so it doesn't squeak all night, dumping the soiled wood chips out of the hamster cage, burying the perished hamster, getting the snow tires put on the car for wintertime damn it, getting the snow tires taken off for summertime damn it, trying at 2:30 a.m. to get back to sleep damn it, trying at 7:00 a.m. to wake up damn it, all the while bottling up eternity inside. Usually we bottle it up pretty well, pretty convincingly, but sometimes in a fever we can feel it.

When I was six I had a fever dream in which I was tasked with memorizing the whole Bible. I remember waking up, scrambling off the bed, staring aghast at the carpet, my brain burning up, and not just from the fever. At the prospect of having to do something I would never be able to do, never and ever got mixed up in my head and I felt the shock of infinity. Even now when I think about that dream, my heart starts to hammer. The boilers-down like to boil things down to their least interesting components—if they boiled me long enough I guess I'd boil down to some gristle, bones, and grease. But all the boiling in the world would never undo the fact that I had once fathomed eternity; that I had once had, as that old song says, "something within me." That something within, "The Kingdom of God is within you"—we felt it in our dreams sometimes, and sometimes in our fevers, and sometimes, holy Moses, you could hear it in our songs.

*

Unconscious goodness is better than conscious goodness. As Mr. Emerson says in *A Room with a View*, "A baby is worth a dozen saints."

Unconscious goodness is better than conscious goodness. Jesus said, "But when you give to the needy, do not let your left hand know what your right hand is doing." The left hand is so gauche, such a blabbermouth. Keep it in your pocket while your right hand is giving some change to the homeless couple outside the gas station.

People who flash their goodness at you. Those people on the internet who indecently expose their righteousness are the same people who indecently expose other people's sins. They are generally exposers, generally indecent, and I hope to never get within a hundred miles of any of them. If you happen to know that one of them is traveling through Bozeman, let me know and I'll truck on over to Sweet Grass County, where there's this countercultural community I like to hang out with, at Greycliff Prairie

Dog Town State Park. Prairie dogs are discreet—I might even say furtive.

People on the internet. Online people get their jollies by surveilling one another. I try mostly to be an offline person, surveilled only by the sun. Well, puppy surveillance is okay too.

"Something within me." If we can have an inner diva to get in touch with, why not an inner buzzard? Why not an inner echidna, an inner aardvark, an inner mesquite, an inner monsoon, an inner asteroid belt (with no discernible purpose)? Why not an inner universe?

"Something within me." The Bee Gees sang about how "the woman in you brings out the man in me" but I like to sing about how "the poodle in you brings out the groomer in me."

The combination of *never* and *ever*. Just as explosive as the combination of nitrated toluene and fuming nitric acid is the combination of *never* and *ever* in the mind.

Fever dream. The same night I dreamed I had to memorize the whole Bible, I also dreamed that someone showed up with a black trash bag full of raw spaghetti with which he was going to poke me. The spaghetti was scary but not as scary as infinity.

Megachurch metric. Megachurches would prefer a ten-pound hummingbird to a 0.056-ounce hummingbird.

Megachurch metric. Megachurches would prefer Neptune to Earth.

Praise Song

The following passage is a bonus excerpt from my forthcoming posthumous memoir, titled "Praise Song."

Before I was born they put Uranus in space and tinted it blue-green and tilted it on its side, and in 1781 they discovered it: "In the quartile near Zeta Tauri the lowest of the two is a curious either nebulous star or perhaps a Comet." They put all those nebulous stars and perhaps-comets out there and made bunnies and sent them hopping around my backyard, so if sometimes I was money-poor, I was never bunny-poor. They made me Romanian breakfasts in Ohio—mamaliga—and saag paneer in Chicago and quinoa stew in Peru, and how frequently I feasted on buttered spaghetti in Texas!

They buttered the spaghetti and bunnied the yard and mooned the sky and grassed the ground and egged the nests and plummed the trees. They sanded the desert and lilied the fields and monkeyed the trees and ottered the streams and fathered and mothered and brothered me, friended and husbanded and babied me, so that although I was many sads in my life—traffic-sad, insomnia-sad, politics-sad—I was many happies too: baby-happy, grass-happy, star-happy. When I looked at the stars I was starstruck, when I looked at the moon I was moonstruck, and when I looked at the Earth I was earthstruck.

I was English-happy, too, because when you put English words together on the page they always started fooling around—praise for rummy, randy, promiscuous English! I was also Spanish-happy because when I learned Spanish I acquired a second, more confident, personality. I liked every language I dabbled in, along with the personalities they imparted. Russian was my sixth language, Greek my fifth, French my fourth, Spanish my third, and English my second. I was an ESL learner all my life because my first language was music.

Praise for the languages and their learnability, praise for the sun and its orbitability, praise for the Earth and its habitability—*O Mamacita Tierra!*—praise for the bread and its butterability, praise for the grapes and their fermentability, praise for the guitars and their rockability, praise for the air and its breathability. If I had had wings I would have been grateful for the air's flyability but I didn't mind being earthbound, even more earthbound than the chickens. Chickens could fly circles around me.

Nobody winged me but they footed and hearted me, tonsilled and kidneyed me, and praise for my fingers and their willability! I considered all my organs saints—Saint Bladder, Saint Brain, Saint Stomach, Saint Pancreas. I think that of all my parts, my elbows were my favorites—good for making space—but I loved my skin, too, because it was so opaque. Blessed are the opaque, for they can choose to hide their insanity, or if they wish they can choose to hide their sanity.

Praise for the bad examples! The bad examples were good examples of what not to be. As canned asparagus taught me to appreciate fresh asparagus, so canned ideas taught me to appreciate fresh ideas. As bland food helped me to appreciate spicy food, so bland books helped me to appreciate spicy books. When I read *The Brothers Karamazov* and the book of Job I wolfed them down—I was a werewolf and my trigger was saltiness, spiciness. But with bland books I was no wolf, just a person deciding she wasn't hungry after all.

They invented me, a werewolf, and made me messy-natured and lazy-natured so that to accomplish anything I had to fight against my nature, so anything I accomplished was a double accomplishment. Praise for my nature and its fightability. They taught me to walk and let me walk off with their hearts, and they were English-happy too—so after they had carried me around in their womb and labored to give birth to me and nursed me and taught me English, word by word, I got wooed by all those books they kept around the house. Though at school my textbooks warned me against literature, the freedom I had at home fortified me against the fortifications I encountered at school.

They never hired me for the jobs for which I interviewed, unless I played the piano. So I never got hired for an academic creative writing position, because they never asked me to play the piano. So I never moved to North Carolina, Massachusetts, or Missouri. I had, however, a hirable husband, who did not have to play the piano to score a job, so we moved to paradise. They made Bozeman the ideal climate for crabapple trees, and one day in September they cut down the crabapple tree in front of my children's elementary school so all the sour little apples were pickable, so we filled up our backpacks, and the next morning they came over with all their applesauce-making equipment and helped me boil, mash, and strain all that fruit into gallons of the reddest, appliest applesauce.

They invented pianos in 1700, instruments that enable the player to be a one-woman band, soloist *and* harmony *and* accompaniment *and* rhythm *and* percussion all at once, and in 1984, they bought me an old upright one for my bedroom. They let me play all night long and raised me in a church that didn't pay its musicians, so I had the opportunity to be a church pianist from a very un-professional age. The first time they gave me money for my music was when I was nine and won ten dollars in a violin vibrato contest, dollars with which I bought a guinea pig. They let me keep him in my room, along with all the hamsters and rabbits and parakeets who put up with my piano playing.

They made hamsters and turtles and buzzards to boot, and hot damn, somebody made some wombats! They made platypuses and blue-footed boobies and morning glories and muons (whatever muons were; they were no doubt important—try imagining a universe without mu-ons!). The unrealistic nature of all those things was the one and only thread I could see tying everything together. If there was just one maker of all those miscellaneous creations, I'd say he or she was primarily unrealistic—muons were unrealistically small, morning glories were unrealistically pretty, platypuses were unrealistically weird, and boobies' feet were unrealistically blue.

By the time I was born, the atmosphere on Earth was crowded with all those ghosts of all those extinct animals—the cave bears and pink-headed ducks and woolly rhinoceroses and laughing owls and pterodactyls and piopios. By 1975 animals were pretty retro. But still the animals who *were* alive were extremely alive, as were the plants—animal alive! plant alive! In Wonderland they played croquet with flamingos for mallets and hedgehogs for balls, and Alice complained, "You've no idea how confusing it is all the things being alive." With all those things being alive, the world was as confusing as Wonderland.

They made scruffy flowers and froufrou flowers and ginger growing gingerly and earthworms gallivanting in the dirt and pikas peeking out of their hidey-holes. I peeked back at the pikas, and once, I saw a woman chasing a dog chasing a cow down a mountain. Looking at some horses by a creek one evening, I saw so many variations of black—glossy blacks and matte blacks and dark blacks and bright blacks. I was not deprived of sight early, like Turlough O'Carolan and that blind boy at camp, or deprived of sight late, like Johann Sebastian Bach and John Milton. I didn't lose my sight on August 21, 2017, because on August 20, 2017, they had thoughtfully left three pairs of eclipse glasses on their front porch for me and my children to use the next day, when we drove to Rexburg, Idaho, to see the sun get mooned. Still, there were so many things I didn't see—the steam ribboning up from my tea in the morning, the moonbow one winter night, eerie-purply-greeny-gold, the angels in the aspen tree, the radishes so red.

I was never ravished by radishes, and I had my reservations about death. But death has made me an appreciator even of radishes, even of the internet, good for stalking wombats. Death is a good foil for the trashiest things—now that I am dead I can even spare a little praise for Walmart. Whenever I went to Walmart they were always out of all seventeen items I needed. It was like they knew I was coming and had announced over the loudspeaker, *Attention, attention, Amy Leach is six minutes away, all workers on hand to unstock the shelves of the following items*, and they rushed around pulling everything I needed off the shelves—the baby socks, buttermilk, licorice, watercolor paints, cucumbers, toddler toothpaste, kosher salt, mint, veggie burgers, sauerkraut, and pickled jalapeños. Thus I always thought that Walmart's slogan should be "Walmart: That Your Misery May Be Complete."

But one time I found mustard greens at Walmart, when I hadn't been able to find them anywhere else. Those mustard greens were mitigating. And one afternoon I locked my keys in the car in the Walmart parking lot when the temperature in Bozeman was minus-thirteen degrees. So I was stuck in the store for two hours, waiting for my ride, and along with the opportunity to not freeze to death, I received a revelation. Previously, I had only ever been looking for the things I was looking for, and because they were never there, I had always felt aggrieved. But that day, on my long walk around Walmart, I realized that although the store did not have the things I was looking for, it was abundantly stocked with things I was not looking for—inflatable bathtub neck pillows and tropical Popsicles and Guinness Baltimore Blonde and misty-scented candles and Minions whistles. After that day I tried more often to look for things I was not looking for, and not just at Walmart.

* * *

When I was four my family lived by a cornfield in Colorado, and I'd watch out our sliding glass doors for a little fist-sized cloud to appear over the mountains. I was watching for one cloud in particular, the one that would grow bigger and brighter and more and more celestial—I was watching for the cloud carrying Jesus and the angels. I'd seen it in Adventist paintings, Jesus standing on the big cottony cloud, impassively holding forth his arms, the homogeneous angels blowing long, skinny trumpets all around him.

Sometimes I'd spy a puffy little candidate floating over the mountains and I'd get very excited, but then it would either dissipate and disappear or come closer and prove to be just a cloud, conveying nobody, and I'd start watching for the next prospect. Because I was only ever looking for a cloud conveying Jesus, I was blind to all the wisping, fluffing, streaking, pinking, superfluous clouds not carrying him. Every day for so many years he did not appear, but at some point in my life I started to wonder if maybe I had been looking for the wrong thing.

I'd never seen Jesus arriving on a cloud, true, but I had never seen him walking away from me, either—not even when my organ playing was disastrous. And there was that one verse where he said, "I am with you always."

Somebody else there was who never walked away. Though my piano renditions of Bach's *Two-Part Inventions* didn't improve after I was about eleven—in fact, I think they got glitchier—the difficulty of playing them was always a motivator, an engine, an invitation. Those pieces took me so much effort, and my playing of them rarely sounded anything other than effortful, hammery. My playing sounded like working. But Difficulty never gave up on me; Difficulty never stopped kicking me in the pants. Like the friendly sparrows said to Peter Rabbit when his coat got snagged on Mr. McGregor's fence, Difficulty said to me, *Exert yourself.*

So I'd sit there at the piano, getting snagged on the notes, exerting myself, and sitting beside me on the piano bench was invariably Difficulty, occasionally Bach, presumably Jesus, and, once, a friend who came over and played those *Inventions* with such invention of her own, taking such liberties with the music—speeding up, slowing down, dropping notes, adding notes—that after I heard her play I started inviting Freedom and Invention to join me, too, while I played those old *Inventions*—to come and sit beside me on the piano bench, along with all my other friends.

PART IV

*

Reprise

＊

Superfluities like pogo, doo-wopping, and dreams. One can forgo the pogo, one can forgo the doo-wopping, but one cannot forgo the dreams.

Nobody going off on tangents. Shakespeare said, "The wiser, the waywarder."

The laundry dancing. Sometimes I call myself an old boot but even old boots can get danced around.

A difference between a grape and a grape. Just as there is a difference between a grape and a grape, so is there is a difference between a smile and a smile. There's the smile before the balloon pops and the smile after the balloon pops.

My gizzard. In my gizzard I feel that Ellen White is no god, because she doesn't put up with any guff. Our days are named for gods, like Wednesday for Woden and Friday for Frigg, and look at all the guff our days put up with! And God the God, he's put up with scribblers like

Gertrude Stein and fiddlers like Scarlet Rivera and loafers like Whitman and dancers like Bunny Briggs and John W. Bubbles.

Frigg. The name *Frigg* and the word *free* come from the same proto-Germanic root word, *frijaz*, which doesn't mean "unencumbered" but "related," and is related to the Sanskrit word for "own, dear, beloved." The more beloveds you have, the freer you are. Dvořák was very free, with his nine children—and with his twenty-two, Bach was even freer.

Frijaz. Just kidding, *frijaz* was invented by Ornette Coleman on his album *The Shape of Jazz to Come*.

In this world you will have trouble. I wonder what Jesus would have said to people who visit the moon. I hear there's trouble there, too, and so to Jesus's statement I would add, *On the moon you will have trouble.*

I was a baby once. Being a baby was new to me, as was being a toddler, a middle-schooler, a teenager, and then being twenty-two, thirty-five, forty-eight, etc.—it was all new. If I get old, being old will be new to me too. Being dead will be new for a little while, then it will get old.

Our transience is our tragedy. I am halfway through my stint as a person and am discovering that age is as heritable as youth.

Our transience is our tragedy. My children were born like fifteen minutes ago and already they are saying things like "I have my doubts about leprechauns."

Our transience is our tragedy. The days are like dominoes, baby—

Our transience is our tragedy. So hop to it!

I just wanna be a sheep, baa baa baa baa. In many ways I do want to be a sheep. I want to be nonviolent, I want to eat grasses and legumes, and I want to possess a stylish appearance.

Muons. There are anti-muons too. I don't know what they are either. Maybe they are folks who march against muons, lobby against muons, write impassioned manifestos against muons.

A one-woman band. I know a bass player named Shawna who is a seven-band woman, because all the bands in Bozeman want her to play with them.

Adventists are heterogeneous. There is a difference between an Adventist and an Adventist. I had some teachers who were coercively Adventist—some who were indoctrinators—and some who were not. In the movie *Things to Come*, the college professor played by Isabelle Huppert meets up with a former student, who censures her for not being true to the Cause—some political Cause, I can't remember which—but she says, No, you've got me wrong; I was only ever trying to get you to think for yourself. I had some teachers like that. There was Mr. Fry, who read us the passage from Genesis about Abraham passing between halved animals, and he asked us what we thought it meant, and because he did not have an answer, because it was a real question, not a fake question, because he actually wanted to know what we thought, I am still thinking about it.

Electrified by a cat. I see this one gray-and-white cat around my neighborhood sometimes. He seems to be his own cat and I'd like to get to know him but he is too cool for me. Come to think of it, a lot of the animals in my neighborhood are cool cats—the deer, magpies, sandhill cranes, pronghorns, and bears. Even the bunnies are too cool for me. My puppy has lower standards.

Insomnia-sad. I am like a sweater that unravels over the course of the day, then at night, sleep knits me back together. When I don't sleep I'm just an unraveled sweater all the time, just a heap of tangled yarn.

I love the Sabbath. I also love that there is no hell in Adventism, or rather it does not involve flames. Going to hell for wearing a pink plastic ring doesn't mean burning forever—just sleeping forever. To the insomniac this doesn't sound too bad, so I wear my pink plastic rings with abandon. However, I think I would be happy in heaven, too, where I assume I'd get to eat forever.

Authority's a pathogen. To qualify: this is true only of *arbitrary* authority. Arbitrary authority is a pathogen for which the cure is experience. When I was young I accepted the arbitrary authorities, but with experience they got sifted out, leaving Emily Dickinson, Glover Wagner, Jesus, and the owls. Compared with spurious authority, real authority is unmistakable.

Children full of beans. My two children came out of nothing not only to totter "on the brink of nothing" like William Hazlitt but also to shriek and giggle and stomp and tussle and throw tantrums and dance to hip-hop music with underpants on their heads on the brink of nothing.

Children full of beans. It is not necessary to have babies! You can leave it to other people! I had a friend in college who was always trying to convince me to have children, but at the time I wasn't interested, so I said, "Have your own damn children." My response to him was similar to my response to people who want *my* book to promote *their* ideologies: write your own damn book.

Selling an Adventist book. I once trained to teach test-preparation classes for Kaplan, and in my presentations I was supposed to plug for Kaplan constantly, as in "And this is why I love the Kaplan method for acing the logic games," and "Here is how Kaplan will help you guess the meaning of 'piquant' successfully." The point seemed to be not test preparation but making people into Kaplanites. Selling Kaplanism felt (exactly) like selling Adventism.

I'm leaster. This is a competition where the wormiest person wins.

An anorexic righteousness. My theory of righteousness and my theory of nutrition are the same: Calories are Good.

"Whatever your hand finds to do, do it with all your might." "Whatever" would include cleaning the toilet, planting the zucchini seeds, pulling the weeds, diapering the baby, shoveling the snow, chopping the onions, even sinning, I suppose. As Martin Luther said, "Love God and sin boldly."

"Hail nothing full of nothing." Before a sinkhole appears in your backyard, you might not think that you need any more space, but *after* the sinkhole appears, you think, "Oh yeah, *wow*, I totally needed that extra space for my dog-piddled couch and warped sandbox and defunct refrigerator and mangled trampoline that got blown into a tree in a windstorm."

My meat is not eating meat. In other words, my meat is eating potatoes.

The difference between the person who exists and the person who does not exist. To my mind, the difference between a being and a nonbeing dwarfs even the differences between species. In the following imperative statements—"Be spaniel," "Be mushroom," "Be person"— which do you think is the most interesting word? To me it is not "spaniel" or "mushroom" or "person" but "be." To be a person or a possum, that is not the question.

To be. An undertaker who read my first book told me I used the verb "to be" too much, that I should vary my verbs more. I was glad for his comment because I hadn't realized I was doing that! I would consider his suggestion! After consideration I decided to continue my practice, albeit consciously, for I find "to be" to be the potentest verb, as undertakers should know.

To be. "To be" is called an auxiliary verb, but I say it's all the other verbs that are auxiliary—schmoozing, boozing, beaning, sponging, sniggering, snogging, dithering, blithering, bellowing, wallowing, harrumphing, pestering, punking, primping, pocketing, plummeting, ribbiting, gibbeting, jabbering, buttering, puttering, petering, muttering, spoofing, splooshing, smooching, etc.—all these activities being auxiliary to being.

To be. Usually I go around thinking sentences with objects, such as: "I hate canned peas," or "I love Willie Nelson," or "I want a llama." But some days my sentences are stripped of all their objects, and I just go around thinking "I hate, I hate," "I love, I love," "I want, I want," "I wish, I wish, I wish," "I am, I am, I am, I am, I am . . ."

The differences between beings. Our little discrepancies allow us to ID one another, and we *love* ID'ing one another! Of course ID'ing people is slightly harder than ID'ing geraniums. To identify a geranium out of the 422 different species of geraniums, you need only determine whether it is herbaceous or succulent, has spiny or smooth stems, whether its flowers are purple-veined, slightly cupped, dark-blotched, etc., and then you can say whether it is a Ballerina or Blue Sunrise or Orion geranium. People are not as readily identifiable. Once, in Lima, I rode in a taxi driven by a man named Geranium, whom I would have identified as a taxi driver. However, he told me he had a Ph.D. in philosophy. Geranium the seeming taxi driver was primarily a philosopher.

ID'ing one another. Just as people love to ID other people, so do they love to ID themselves. I have known more than a few people who identified as God.

Memoir school. When I was in graduate school the coolest thing for a writer to be was *transgressive*. But now, twenty years on, it seems like writers are praised more for being *responsible*. Transgressive is out; responsible is in. Oh, the vicissitudes of cool.

The vicissitudes of cool. I recently read a newspaper article about how hard it is to know which jeans are cool anymore, because, as the author fretted, "there's no consensus on jeans these days." It is so upsetting when there is no consensus on something! How are we to know which jeans to buy or novels to read or sandwiches to eat or thoughts to think? In the absence of consensus, we wish a queen would take over and issue decrees so there would be no question about what we should be wearing, saying, drinking, thinking.

The vicissitudes of cool. Having cool jeans is like having a cool car or cool opinions: you can possess them and still not be very smart. I don't know if my Honda is cool or uncool but I do know that it does not enhance my intelligence. On the other hand my Ford F-150 definitely enhances my visibility: I used to feel invisible until I started driving a big red pickup truck.

My affiliation is not denominational. Actually, I did join a Congregational church a few years ago, a church in which God does not play second banana to a dead little fussbudget. In the Congregational church, individuals are not only *permitted* but *expected* to exercise their freedom of conscience.

Jellyfish memoirs being ruled out. Most jellyfish die before they get old enough to write mature memoirs, so I say let them go ahead and write immature memoirs. The exception would be the immortal jellyfish, who could accumulate centuries of experience before writing her memoir, unless she gets eaten by a sea turtle first and becomes a mortal jellyfish.

People on the internet. Inhabitants of the internet are always having a cow. Some of them even manage to have several cows per day. The internet is quite a cow factory.

Cow factory. The internet is also a star factory! Look at all those proliferating stars of opinion! To my mind there is just one thing missing from the internet: a website where you can rate the stars. It doesn't seem right for them to go unrated, as if they were exempt from opinion. So here's what I'm going to do: I'm going to start a website where you can give that dinky pale-green Zubeneschamali one star and the sparkly ruby Antares four and a half stars. There will be aggregate ratings, there will be two-star stars and three-star stars and five-star stars, and with the addition of my website, the internet will be complete.

A one-theory ethnographer. I'd probably even apply my theory to the stars: stars are like people too. As George Herbert wrote, "Stars have their storms, ev'n in a high degree / As well as we." Stars—they're just like us!

A man named Reindeer. I have heard of a man named Turnip but I've never met a woman named Omelette, which is odd, because it is really a romantic name.

My followers. My followers used to all be dogs, and I spoke mostly gibberish. After children started following me around, I had to start speaking English all day long. It is a lot of work. Gibberish comes far more naturally to me.

An unyammy yam. An unyammy yam is like an unblobby blob. Unblobby blobs give me the creeps.

Musical terms in Latin. *Quasi allegro* means "almost happy," and *quasi allegretto* means "almost little-happy," and *quasi alligator* means "almost alligator."

Time's a tyrant. Or time can be a game, as Heraclitus writes:

> *Time is a game*
> *played beautifully*
> *by children.*

Iconoclasts. It has always seemed funny to me that the founders of Adventism were extolled for *not accepting* the dogma they had inherited, for reading, praying, and thinking for themselves, while the inheritors of *their* ideas were supposed to only accept, submit, defer, obey. Iconoclasm is for me, not for thee.

"He maketh his sun to rise on the evil and on the good and sendeth rain on the just and on the unjust." The indifference of nature is often said to be cruel, but nature is not just indifferently *cruel* but also indifferently *beneficent*—sunny, rainy, moony, birdy, lilacky, Juney. Imagine nature was a stickler and you could hear the robins yeeping and chucking only if you had attended Sabbath School, or the guppy would opalesce for you only if you had passed out evangelistic tracts, and creeks would splash your hot feet only if you had paid your tithe. But nature and God are not partisan like people.

One maker of all those miscellaneous creations. I'm a monotheist because of that trippy thought—that such variety could proceed from one mind. I am a monotheist like Akhenaten, although, of course, in his day monotheism was criminalized. Monotheism was his marijuana.

Such variety proceeding from one mind. God is like William Shakespeare, God is like Johann Sebastian Bach, God is like Emily Dickinson.

Monotheism. I am a monotheist but a polydoggist and a polypiggist and a polypantherist and also a polypreacherist. Listen to two different preachers talking about the same verse: One manipulates the text to suit his dogma, while the other follows it wherever it goes. The first runs around in tiny little circles behind the pulpit, while the second runs all over the universe. There he is now (Glover Wagner), rounding the Pleiades.

A polydoggist. The monodoggist says, *There is no dog but dog.* The polydoggist believes in a panoply of dogs. The only problem with panoplies is that whenever there is more than one of something, hierarchy sets in. I've seen a sign in Yellowstone depicting a schnauzer with a line crossed through it: "No Schnauzers." It is sad to think of all those schnauzers sitting at home while the boxers and beagles and chow chows are whooping it up in the park.

"No Schnauzers." Where this rule leaves schnoodles and schnorkies, I am not sure.

Pedal damn it. I used to not "pedal damn it" but "pedal sort of" because I bought a road bike that went *faster-and-faster-and-faster-and-faster*, whether I pedaled or not. Compared with the heavy Huffy of my tweens, this bicycle was a perpetual motion machine, requiring practically no external force, and I was terrified of it. At night I'd lie in bed and imagine crashing into trees and cars and pedestrians. This went on for a few months, my bicycle dread, until one day on the trail through the Chicago forest I rode up behind a man, who, in getting onto his bike, wobbled over into the passing lane, and I crashed into him. We tumbled into a heap and I sobbed and blubbered and hugged him, and after that I was no longer afraid of crashing. Crashing cured me of my fear of crashing. I wonder if it will be the same with dying.

They grassed the ground. Grass is so very becoming to the ground.

Duck writers. I would like to read a book written by a duck.

Forte is their forte. Like the baby who lives across the street from me. As soon as he could crawl, he'd crawl over to the stereo and turn the volume all the way up. That baby is right—the only problem with most music is that it's not loud enough! If you don't like a song, just turn it up! It can work for books, too, like if you didn't like this book, try reading it again but out loud, as loud as you can. Though if you still don't like my book after shouting it to yourself, that's okay, I understand. Sometimes I am not on my own wavelength either.

Somebody made some wombats. How fanciful is a wombat! How fanciful is a person! How fanciful we must appear to the stones, we Edwards and Howards going backwards and forwards. To the stone, the geologist must seem so fanciful, with all her volition. Of course the six-year-old geologist has not yet forgotten how fanciful he is, or how fanciful everything is. Sometimes he puts on swim goggles and takes a hammer to the stones, smashing into their fancifully sparkly hearts.

Somebody made some wombats. The maker of wombats—someone who expresses himself in wombats—now there's a god I can get behind!

A pushy prophet. To Ellen White, as to other pushy people, I say, *Back off, lady*, but I never say that to God, because God is not officious. To God I say, *Thank you for the stars*. I asked him for the answers but he gave me the stars so I say, *Thank you for the stars*.

Acknowledgments

Thank you to Mary Margaret Alvarado, Sean Hopkinson, Mindy Misener, Scott Parker, Jody Hechtman, Todd Hechtman, Dan Lamberton, Jerry Burr, and Joni Tevis for reading my book early on and sharing your wisdom. I treasure such wisdom, such friendship.

Thank you to Jin Auh for tremendous help and vision all along the way. Thank you to Jenna Johnson for brilliant ideas and tireless support.

Thank you to my parents for lighting up my way. Thank you to Matthew for never-ending patience and encouragement.

Thank you to Peter and Sylvie, the saltiest people I know, for the joy, joy, joy, joy down in my heart.

Amy Leach is the author of *The Everybody Ensemble* and *Things That Are*. She grew up in Texas and earned her MFA from the Nonfiction Writing Program at the University of Iowa. Her work has appeared in *The Best American Essays*, *The Best American Science and Nature Writing*, and numerous other publications, including *Granta*, *A Public Space*, *Orion*, *Tin House*, and the *Los Angeles Review of Books*. She is a recipient of a Whiting Award, a Rona Jaffe Foundation Writers' Award, and a Pushcart Prize. Leach lives in Montana.